Table Of Contents

Did You Know? Fascinating Facts and Trivia for Curious Minds

Chapter 1: History

Fun Facts About History

1. The shortest war in history was between Britain and Zanzibar on August 27, 1896. It lasted only 38 minutes.
2. Cleopatra lived closer in time to the moon landing than to the construction of the Great Pyramid of Giza.
3. In 1815, the eruption of Mount Tambora in Indonesia caused the "Year Without a Summer," leading to global food shortages.
4. The Eiffel Tower was originally meant to be a temporary structure for the 1889 World's Fair in Paris.
5. The Great Fire of London in 1666 destroyed 80% of the city but caused surprisingly few deaths.

Trivia Quiz Part 1: History

1. **What year did the Berlin Wall fall?**
   A. 1969
   B. 1989
   C. 1991
   D. 1975
2. **Which civilisation is credited with inventing the wheel?**
   A. Egyptians
   B. Sumerians
   C. Greeks
   D. Romans
3. **Who was the first President of the United States?**
   A. Thomas Jefferson
   B. George Washington
   C. Abraham Lincoln
   D. Benjamin Franklin
4. **What was the name of the ship that famously sank in 1912?**
   A. Lusitania
   B. Britannic
   C. Titanic
   D. Queen Mary
5. **Which empire was known as "The Land of the Rising Sun"?**
   A. Ottoman Empire
   B. Byzantine Empire
   C. Japanese Empire
   D. Mongol Empire

6. True or False: The Roman Empire lasted over 1,000 years.

7. Who wrote the famous diary documenting life during World War II?
   A. Helen Keller
   B. Anne Frank
   C. Winston Churchill
   D. Eleanor Roosevelt

8. Which event is often considered the start of World War II?
   A. The assassination of Archduke Franz Ferdinand
   B. The signing of the Treaty of Versailles
   C. Germany's invasion of Poland
   D. Japan's attack on Pearl Harbor

9. What ancient structure in Rome could hold up to 50,000 spectators?
   A. The Colosseum
   B. The Parthenon
   C. The Pantheon
   D. Circus Maximus

10. Which famous explorer was the first European to reach India by sea?
    A. Christopher Columbus
    B. Ferdinand Magellan
    C. Vasco da Gama
    D. Marco Polo

Answers Part 1: History

1. B. 1989
2. B. Sumerians
3. B. George Washington
4. C. Titanic
5. C. Japanese Empire
6. True
7. B. Anne Frank
8. C. Germany's invasion of Poland
9. A. The Colosseum
10. C. Vasco da Gama

More Fun Facts About History

1. Napoleon Bonaparte was once attacked by a horde of rabbits during a hunting trip. His staff had gathered tame rabbits for him to hunt, but they overwhelmed him instead.
2. The Great Wall of China is not a single continuous wall, but a series of walls and fortifications built over centuries by various Chinese dynasties.
3. The Boston Tea Party of 1773 was not just about tea—it was a protest against British taxation policies, especially the Tea Act.
4. During World War II, British intelligence used Monopoly games to smuggle maps, compasses, and escape tools to Allied prisoners of war.
5. The first written peace treaty in history, the Treaty of Kadesh, was signed between the Egyptians and the Hittites in 1259 BCE.

Trivia Quiz Part 2: History

1. **Which explorer was credited with discovering America in 1492?**
   A. Ferdinand Magellan
   B. Christopher Columbus
   C. Leif Erikson
   D. Vasco da Gama
2. **What year did the French Revolution begin?**
   A. 1789
   B. 1776
   C. 1799
   D. 1801
3. **Which British monarch had the longest reign before Queen Elizabeth II?**
   A. Queen Victoria
   B. King George III
   C. Queen Mary I
   D. King Edward VII
4. **What was the name of the first human civilisation in Mesopotamia?**
   A. Babylon
   B. Sumer
   C. Assyria
   D. Akkad
5. **The Magna Carta, signed in 1215, limited the power of which English king?**
   A. King Henry VIII
   B. King Richard I
   C. King John
   D. King Edward III

6. **True or False: The American Civil War ended in 1863.**

7. **Which city was known as Byzantium before becoming Constantinople and later Istanbul?**
   A. Athens
   B. Rome
   C. Troy
   D. Byzantium

8. **Who was the first woman to win a Nobel Prize?**
   A. Marie Curie
   B. Florence Nightingale
   C. Rosalind Franklin
   D. Ada Lovelace

9. **What ancient artifact helped scholars decipher Egyptian hieroglyphs?**
   A. The Dead Sea Scrolls
   B. The Rosetta Stone
   C. The Code of Hammurabi
   D. The Cyrus Cylinder

10. **What event marked the end of the Middle Ages in Europe?**
    A. The signing of the Magna Carta
    B. The fall of Constantinople
    C. The discovery of America
    D. The invention of the printing press

11. **Which famous ruler declared, "I am the state"?**
    A. Napoleon Bonaparte
    B. Louis XIV of France
    C. Julius Caesar
    D. Peter the Great

12. **Who was assassinated in Sarajevo in 1914, sparking World War I?**
    A. Franz Ferdinand
    B. Gavrilo Princip
    C. Wilhelm II
    D. Archduke Charles
13. **What was the longest dynasty in Chinese history?**
    A. Ming
    B. Zhou
    C. Tang
    D. Qin
14. **Which revolutionary leader famously rode a horse named Bucephalus?**
    A. Alexander the Great
    B. Genghis Khan
    C. Attila the Hun
    D. Charlemagne
15. **Which country gifted the Statue of Liberty to the United States?**
    A. France
    B. England
    C. Germany
    D. Spain

Answers Part 2: History

1. B. Christopher Columbus
2. A. 1789
3. A. Queen Victoria
4. B. Sumer
5. C. King John
6. False (The American Civil War ended in 1865.)
7. D. Byzantium
8. A. Marie Curie
9. B. The Rosetta Stone
10. B. The fall of Constantinople
11. B. Louis XIV of France
12. A. Franz Ferdinand
13. B. Zhou
14. A. Alexander the Great
15. A. France

Trivia Quiz Part 3: History

1. **Which empire was known for building a network of roads that stretched over 40,000 kilometres?**
    A. Roman Empire
    B. Persian Empire
    C. Inca Empire
    D. Mongol Empire
2. **Who was the first ruler to unify China under one empire?**
    A. Liu Bang
    B. Qin Shi Huang
    C. Wu Zetian
    D. Sun Tzu
3. **What year did the Titanic begin its ill-fated voyage?**
    A. 1910
    B. 1911
    C. 1912
    D. 1913
4. **Which pharaoh was responsible for the construction of the Great Pyramid of Giza?**
    A. Tutankhamun
    B. Khufu
    C. Ramses II
    D. Akhenaten

5. **True or False: The Renaissance began in Spain.**
6. **Which country was the first to grant women the right to vote?**
   A. United States
   B. New Zealand
   C. Finland
   D. Canada
7. **Who led the Haitian Revolution, which resulted in the first independent, Black-led republic?**
   A. Jean-Jacques Dessalines
   B. Toussaint Louverture
   C. Henri Christophe
   D. Marcus Garvey
8. **What historical event is depicted in Pablo Picasso's painting *Guernica*?**
   A. The Spanish Civil War
   B. World War I
   C. The French Revolution
   D. The Russian Revolution
9. **Which explorer was the first to circumnavigate the globe?**
   A. Ferdinand Magellan
   B. Christopher Columbus
   C. Vasco da Gama
   D. Sir Francis Drake
10. **What ancient wonder of the world was located in Babylon?**
    A. The Great Pyramid of Giza
    B. The Hanging Gardens
    C. The Temple of Artemis
    D. The Lighthouse of Alexandria

11. **What ancient battle is known for the heroic last stand of 300 Spartans?**
    A. Battle of Thermopylae
    B. Battle of Marathon
    C. Battle of Salamis
    D. Battle of Plataea

12. **Who became the first democratically elected president of South Africa in 1994?**
    A. Desmond Tutu
    B. F.W. de Klerk
    C. Nelson Mandela
    D. Thabo Mbeki

13. **Which treaty ended World War I?**
    A. Treaty of Versailles
    B. Treaty of Tordesillas
    C. Treaty of Paris
    D. Treaty of Ghent

14. **Who was the longest-reigning monarch in British history?**
    A. Queen Elizabeth II
    B. Queen Victoria
    C. King George III
    D. King Henry VIII

15. **What was the name of the famous Berlin airport that served as a base for the Berlin Airlift during the Cold War?**
    A. Tegel Airport
    B. Tempelhof Airport
    C. Schönefeld Airport
    D. Brandenburg Airport

Answers Part 3: History

1. A. Roman Empire
2. B. Qin Shi Huang
3. C. 1912
4. B. Khufu
5. False (The Renaissance began in Italy.)
6. B. New Zealand
7. B. Toussaint Louverture
8. A. The Spanish Civil War
9. A. Ferdinand Magellan
10. B. The Hanging Gardens
11. A. Battle of Thermopylae
12. C. Nelson Mandela
13. A. Treaty of Versailles
14. A. Queen Elizabeth II
15. B. Tempelhof Airport

Chapter 2: Science

Fun Facts About Science

1. A teaspoon of a neutron star would weigh about 6 billion tons on Earth due to its extreme density.
2. Water can boil and freeze at the same time under the right conditions, a phenomenon called the "triple point."
3. Octopuses have three hearts, and two of them stop beating when they swim.
4. The DNA in your body, if uncoiled, could stretch from the Sun to Pluto and back—17 times.
5. Honey never spoils; archaeologists have found pots of honey in ancient Egyptian tombs that are still edible.

Trivia Quiz Part 1: Science

1. What is the chemical symbol for gold?
   A. Gd
   B. Au
   C. Ag
   D. Go
2. What planet in our solar system is known as the "Red Planet"?
   A. Venus
   B. Mars
   C. Jupiter
   D. Mercury

3. **What gas do plants primarily use during photosynthesis?**
   A. Oxygen
   B. Nitrogen
   C. Carbon dioxide
   D. Hydrogen
4. **Who is credited with developing the laws of motion and universal gravitation?**
   A. Galileo Galilei
   B. Isaac Newton
   C. Albert Einstein
   D. Nikola Tesla
5. **True or False: Lightning is hotter than the surface of the Sun.**
6. **Which element is the most abundant in the universe?**
   A. Hydrogen
   B. Oxygen
   C. Carbon
   D. Helium
7. **What part of the brain is responsible for regulating balance and coordination?**
   A. Cerebrum
   B. Medulla
   C. Cerebellum
   D. Hypothalamus
8. **What is the only metal that is liquid at room temperature?**
   A. Mercury
   B. Gallium
   C. Lead
   D. Tin

9. What is the name of the first artificial satellite launched into space?
   A. Apollo 11
   B. Sputnik 1
   C. Voyager 1
   D. Luna 2
10. What type of scientist studies earthquakes?
    A. Meteorologist
    B. Geologist
    C. Seismologist
    D. Volcanologist

Answers Part 1: Science

1. B. Au
2. B. Mars
3. C. Carbon dioxide
4. B. Isaac Newton
5. True
6. A. Hydrogen
7. C. Cerebellum
8. A. Mercury
9. B. Sputnik 1
10. C. Seismologist

More Fun Facts About Science

1. Bananas are radioactive because they contain potassium-40, a naturally occurring isotope.
2. The speed of light is approximately 299,792 kilometres per second (or 186,282 miles per second).
3. Sharks existed before trees—they've been around for over 400 million years.
4. Antarctica is the driest, windiest, and coldest continent, but it is technically a desert.
5. The human body replaces about 98% of its atoms every year through natural biological processes.
6. Saturn's moon Titan is the only celestial body, other than Earth, known to have rivers and lakes, though they're made of liquid methane and ethane.
7. Hot water freezes faster than cold water under certain conditions, a phenomenon known as the Mpemba effect.
8. The Great Barrier Reef is the largest living structure on Earth and is visible from space.
9. There are more trees on Earth than stars in the Milky Way galaxy—about 3 trillion trees compared to 100–400 billion stars.
10. The largest volcano in the solar system is Olympus Mons on Mars, which is nearly three times the height of Mount Everest.

Trivia Quiz Part 2: Science

1. **What is the most common blood type in humans?**
   A. A+
   B. O+
   C. AB-
   D. B-
2. **What is the smallest unit of life?**
   A. Molecule
   B. Atom
   C. Cell
   D. Organ
3. **What force keeps planets in orbit around the Sun?**
   A. Magnetism
   B. Gravity
   C. Friction
   D. Centripetal force
4. **Who developed the periodic table of elements?**
   A. Dmitri Mendeleev
   B. Marie Curie
   C. John Dalton
   D. Ernest Rutherford
5. **True or False: Sound travels faster in water than in air.**
6. **What is the name of the galaxy closest to the Milky Way?**
   A. Andromeda
   B. Triangulum
   C. Sombrero
   D. Whirlpool

7. What is the primary component of natural gas?
   A. Propane
   B. Butane
   C. Methane
   D. Ethanol
8. Which branch of science studies fossils and ancient life forms?
   A. Geology
   B. Paleontology
   C. Archaeology
   D. Anthropology
9. What is the term for an organism that can make its own food using sunlight?
   A. Heterotroph
   B. Autotroph
   C. Decomposer
   D. Herbivore
10. What is the powerhouse of the cell?
    A. Nucleus
    B. Ribosome
    C. Mitochondrion
    D. Endoplasmic reticulum
11. What natural phenomenon is measured by the Richter scale?
    A. Tornado intensity
    B. Earthquake magnitude
    C. Hurricane speed
    D. Tsunami height

12. What is the freezing point of water in Fahrenheit?
    A. 0°F
    B. 32°F
    C. 100°F
    D. -32°F
13. Who proposed the heliocentric theory, which states that the planets revolve around the Sun?
    A. Nicolaus Copernicus
    B. Galileo Galilei
    C. Johannes Kepler
    D. Tycho Brahe
14. What is the term for animals that are active during the night?
    A. Diurnal
    B. Crepuscular
    C. Nocturnal
    D. Arboreal
15. What is the process called when a solid turns directly into a gas?
    A. Melting
    B. Condensation
    C. Sublimation
    D. Deposition

Answers Part 2: Science

1. B. O+
2. C. Cell
3. B. Gravity
4. A. Dmitri Mendeleev
5. True
6. A. Andromeda
7. C. Methane
8. B. Paleontology
9. B. Autotroph
10. C. Mitochondrion
11. B. Earthquake magnitude
12. B. 32°F
13. A. Nicolaus Copernicus
14. C. Nocturnal
15. C. Sublimation

Even More Fun Facts About Science

1. A day on Venus is longer than a year on Venus. It takes about 243 Earth days to rotate once on its axis but only 225 Earth days to complete one orbit around the Sun.
2. Humans share about 60% of their DNA with bananas and approximately 98% with chimpanzees.
3. The Amazon rainforest produces 20% of the world's oxygen and is often referred to as the "lungs of the planet."
4. Light can travel around the Earth 7.5 times in just one second.
5. There are more atoms in a glass of water than there are glasses of water in all the oceans on Earth.
6. The coldest temperature ever recorded on Earth was -128.6°F (-89.2°C) in Antarctica at the Soviet Union's Vostok Station in 1983.
7. Birds are directly descended from dinosaurs, making modern birds technically a type of dinosaur.
8. A blue whale's heart is so large that a human could swim through its arteries.
9. Jellyfish have existed for over 500 million years, outliving dinosaurs and surviving multiple mass extinction events.
10. The observable universe is estimated to be 93 billion light-years in diameter, though it's still expanding.

Trivia Quiz Part 3: Science

1. **What is the most abundant gas in Earth's atmosphere?**
   A. Oxygen
   B. Nitrogen
   C. Carbon dioxide
   D. Hydrogen
2. **Which planet has the largest volcano in the solar system?**
   A. Earth
   B. Venus
   C. Mars
   D. Jupiter
3. **What type of blood cells help fight infections?**
   A. Red blood cells
   B. Platelets
   C. White blood cells
   D. Plasma cells
4. **Which scientist is credited with discovering penicillin?**
   A. Louis Pasteur
   B. Alexander Fleming
   C. Edward Jenner
   D. Joseph Lister
5. **True or False: Humans can survive without a spleen.**
6. **What is the name of the scale used to measure the hardness of minerals?**
   A. Richter scale
   B. Mohs scale
   C. Kelvin scale
   D. Beaufort scale

7. **What is the largest organ in the human body?**
   A. Liver
   B. Brain
   C. Skin
   D. Heart
8. **What is the name of the particle that carries a negative charge in an atom?**
   A. Proton
   B. Electron
   C. Neutron
   D. Positron
9. **What is the term for the amount of matter in an object?**
   A. Volume
   B. Mass
   C. Density
   D. Weight
10. **Which planet is known for having the most moons in the solar system?**
    A. Jupiter
    B. Saturn
    C. Uranus
    D. Neptune
11. **What is the branch of science that studies sound called?**
    A. Optics
    B. Acoustics
    C. Thermodynamics
    D. Mechanics

12. **What natural phenomenon is caused by the sudden release of energy in the Earth's crust?**
    A. Tornado
    B. Tsunami
    C. Earthquake
    D. Landslide
13. **Who is known as the "Father of Modern Physics"?**
    A. Albert Einstein
    B. Galileo Galilei
    C. Max Planck
    D. Isaac Newton
14. **What is the closest star to Earth?**
    A. Proxima Centauri
    B. Sirius
    C. Alpha Centauri
    D. The Sun
15. **What is the study of weather called?**
    A. Astronomy
    B. Meteorology
    C. Geology
    D. Climatology

Answers Part 3: Science

1. B. Nitrogen
2. C. Mars
3. C. White blood cells
4. B. Alexander Fleming
5. True
6. B. Mohs scale
7. C. Skin
8. B. Electron
9. B. Mass
10. B. Saturn
11. B. Acoustics
12. C. Earthquake
13. A. Albert Einstein
14. D. The Sun
15. B. Meteorology

Chapter 3: Biology

Fun Facts About Biology

1. The human brain has about 86 billion neurons, each capable of forming thousands of connections, making it one of the most complex structures in the universe.
2. Starfish don't have brains but use a complex nervous system to sense and respond to their environment.
3. The blue whale is the largest animal on Earth, growing up to 98 feet long and weighing as much as 200 tons.
4. A single strand of human DNA, if stretched out, would measure about 6 feet long.
5. The heart of a hummingbird beats up to 1,260 times per minute during flight.
6. Cockroaches can survive for up to a week without their heads because their brains are not essential for basic functions.
7. The human stomach produces a new lining every three to four days to protect itself from its acidic digestive juices.
8. Platypuses are one of the few mammals that lay eggs and have venomous spurs on their hind legs.
9. Some trees, like the bristlecone pine, can live for over 5,000 years, making them the longest-living organisms on Earth.
10. Your body contains more bacteria than human cells, with the ratio being about 1.3 bacterial cells for every human cell.

Trivia Quiz Part 1: Biology

1. **What is the smallest bone in the human body?**
   A. Femur
   B. Stapes
   C. Radius
   D. Ulna
2. **What type of blood vessel carries blood away from the heart?**
   A. Vein
   B. Artery
   C. Capillary
   D. Lymphatic vessel
3. **What is the process by which plants make food using sunlight?**
   A. Respiration
   B. Photosynthesis
   C. Fermentation
   D. Metabolism
4. **True or False: All mammals have hair or fur.**
5. **What is the powerhouse of the cell?**
   A. Nucleus
   B. Ribosome
   C. Mitochondrion
   D. Endoplasmic reticulum
6. **Which organ in the human body is responsible for filtering blood?**
   A. Liver
   B. Kidneys
   C. Lungs
   D. Spleen

7. Which animal has the largest brain in proportion to its body size?
   A. Elephant
   B. Dolphin
   C. Octopus
   D. Human

8. What pigment gives plants their green colour?
   A. Melanin
   B. Chlorophyll
   C. Haemoglobin
   D. Xanthophyll

9. What is the main function of red blood cells?
   A. To fight infections
   B. To carry oxygen
   C. To produce hormones
   D. To clot blood

10. What is the term for an animal that eats both plants and animals?
    A. Herbivore
    B. Carnivore
    C. Omnivore
    D. Detritivore

11. What part of a plant is responsible for absorbing water and nutrients?
    A. Leaves
    B. Stems
    C. Roots
    D. Flowers

12. What is the name of the largest internal organ in the human body?
    A. Heart
    B. Liver
    C. Brain
    D. Intestines

13. **Which type of blood cell is involved in clotting?**
    A. Red blood cells
    B. Platelets
    C. White blood cells
    D. Plasma
14. **What animal can regenerate its limbs if they are lost?**
    A. Starfish
    B. Snake
    C. Frog
    D. Penguin
15. **What is the primary component of human hair and nails?**
    A. Collagen
    B. Keratin
    C. Elastin
    D. Chitin

Answers Part 1: Biology

1. B. Stapes
2. B. Artery
3. B. Photosynthesis
4. True
5. C. Mitochondrion
6. B. Kidneys
7. D. Human
8. B. Chlorophyll
9. B. To carry oxygen
10. C. Omnivore
11. C. Roots
12. B. Liver
13. B. Platelets
14. A. Starfish
15. B. Keratin

More Fun Facts About Biology

1. The human nose can detect about 1 trillion different scents, far more than previously thought.
2. Axolotls, a type of salamander, can regenerate not only their limbs but also parts of their heart, brain, and spinal cord.
3. The tardigrade, also known as the "water bear," is one of the most resilient creatures on Earth. It can survive extreme temperatures, radiation, and even the vacuum of space.

4. Sloths only defecate about once a week and are highly vulnerable to predators during this time.
5. The fingerprints of a koala are so similar to humans that they have been confused at crime scenes.
6. The ostrich's eye is larger than its brain, making it one of the few animals with this unique feature.
7. The Greenland shark can live for over 400 years, making it the longest-living vertebrate on the planet.
8. The largest flower in the world, the Rafflesia arnoldii, can grow up to 3 feet in diameter and smells like rotting flesh to attract flies for pollination.
9. Some species of jellyfish are considered biologically immortal, as they can revert to earlier stages of their life cycle under stress.
10. The smallest bird in the world, the bee hummingbird, weighs less than a penny.

Trivia Quiz Part 2: Biology

1. **What is the study of fungi called?**
   A. Botany
   B. Mycology
   C. Zoology
   D. Ecology
2. **Which organ in the human body stores bile?**
   A. Liver
   B. Gallbladder
   C. Pancreas
   D. Stomach
3. **What type of symmetry do starfish have?**
   A. Bilateral
   B. Radial
   C. Asymmetrical
   D. Linear
4. **True or False: The human body contains more bones at birth than in adulthood.**
5. **Which blood type is considered the universal donor?**
   A. A+
   B. AB-
   C. O-
   D. B+
6. **What is the name of the pigment that determines skin colour in humans?**
   A. Chlorophyll
   B. Melanin
   C. Haemoglobin
   D. Xanthophyll

7. **What is the term for a group of lions?**
   A. Flock
   B. Herd
   C. Pride
   D. Pack
8. **Which human organ is responsible for producing insulin?**
   A. Liver
   B. Pancreas
   C. Kidneys
   D. Spleen
9. **What is the main component of a plant's cell wall?**
   A. Keratin
   B. Cellulose
   C. Starch
   D. Chitin
10. **Which part of the brain controls involuntary actions like breathing and heartbeat?**
    A. Cerebrum
    B. Cerebellum
    C. Medulla oblongata
    D. Hypothalamus
11. **What is the term for animals that eat only plants?**
    A. Carnivores
    B. Omnivores
    C. Herbivores
    D. Detritivores
12. **Which mammal is known for laying eggs?**
    A. Echidna
    B. Platypus
    C. Both A and B
    D. None of the above

13. **What type of cells are responsible for transmitting signals in the human nervous system?**
    A. Neurons
    B. Erythrocytes
    C. Leukocytes
    D. Thrombocytes
14. **What is the largest bone in the human body?**
    A. Humerus
    B. Tibia
    C. Femur
    D. Radius
15. **What is the term for a plant that lives for more than two years?**
    A. Annual
    B. Biennial
    C. Perennial
    D. Seasonal

Answers Part 2: Biology

1. B. Mycology
2. B. Gallbladder
3. B. Radial
4. True (Babies have about 270 bones, which fuse to 206 by adulthood.)
5. C. O-
6. B. Melanin
7. C. Pride
8. B. Pancreas
9. B. Cellulose
10. C. Medulla oblongata
11. C. Herbivores
12. C. Both A and B
13. A. Neurons
14. C. Femur
15. C. Perennial

Chapter 4: Physics

Fun Facts About Physics

1. If you could fold a piece of paper 42 times, it would reach the Moon. This is due to exponential growth, as the thickness doubles with each fold.
2. A lightning bolt is five times hotter than the surface of the Sun, reaching temperatures of up to 30,000 Kelvin.
3. Black holes can slow down time due to their immense gravitational pull, a phenomenon predicted by Einstein's theory of general relativity.
4. The speed of sound is slower in air than in water; in fact, sound travels about 4.3 times faster in water than in air.
5. If you drop a feather and a hammer on the Moon, they'll hit the ground at the same time because there's no air resistance.
6. Light can behave both as a particle and as a wave, a duality that is a cornerstone of quantum physics.
7. Absolute zero, the lowest theoretical temperature, is -273.15°C (-459.67°F), where all atomic motion theoretically stops.
8. The Large Hadron Collider (LHC) near Geneva is the world's largest and most powerful particle accelerator, with a circumference of 27 kilometres.
9. A day on Jupiter lasts only about 10 hours because of its rapid rotation, despite being the largest planet in the solar system.

10. The concept of gravity was first mathematically described by Isaac Newton, but Albert Einstein expanded our understanding of it as the curvature of spacetime.

Trivia Quiz Part 1: Physics

1. **What is the unit of force in the International System of Units (SI)?**
   A. Joule
   B. Newton
   C. Watt
   D. Pascal
2. **What is the speed of light in a vacuum?**
   A. 3,000 m/s
   B. 30,000 km/s
   C. 300,000 km/s
   D. 3,000,000 km/s
3. **What is the term for the resistance of an object to changes in its state of motion?**
   A. Momentum
   B. Inertia
   C. Acceleration
   D. Friction
4. **True or False: Sound cannot travel through a vacuum.**
5. **Which scientist proposed the three laws of motion?**
   A. Galileo Galilei
   B. Albert Einstein
   C. Isaac Newton
   D. Johannes Kepler

6. **What phenomenon causes a straw in a glass of water to appear bent?**
   A. Reflection
   B. Refraction
   C. Diffraction
   D. Absorption
7. **What type of energy is stored in an object due to its position or height?**
   A. Kinetic energy
   B. Potential energy
   C. Thermal energy
   D. Electrical energy
8. **What is the name of the force that opposes the motion of an object through air?**
   A. Gravity
   B. Friction
   C. Air resistance
   D. Drag
9. **What is the term for the splitting of a nucleus into smaller nuclei, releasing energy?**
   A. Fusion
   B. Fission
   C. Ionisation
   D. Radiation
10. **What type of wave is light?**
    A. Sound wave
    B. Longitudinal wave
    C. Electromagnetic wave
    D. Mechanical wave

11. **What is the first law of thermodynamics?**
    A. Energy cannot be destroyed but can be created.
    B. Energy cannot be created or destroyed, only transformed.
    C. Entropy of the universe always increases.
    D. Energy always moves from hot to cold objects.
12. **What is the term for the natural frequency at which an object vibrates?**
    A. Harmonic frequency
    B. Resonance
    C. Amplitude
    D. Wave frequency
13. **What is the smallest particle of an element that retains its properties?**
    A. Molecule
    B. Atom
    C. Proton
    D. Electron
14. **Who is known as the "Father of Quantum Physics"?**
    A. Niels Bohr
    B. Werner Heisenberg
    C. Max Planck
    D. Richard Feynman
15. **What is the gravitational acceleration on Earth?**
    A. $5.8 \ m/s^2$
    B. $8.9 \ m/s^2$
    C. $9.8 \ m/s^2$
    D. $10.2 \ m/s^2$

Answers Part 1: Physics

1. B. Newton
2. C. 300,000 km/s
3. B. Inertia
4. True
5. C. Isaac Newton
6. B. Refraction
7. B. Potential energy
8. D. Drag
9. B. Fission
10. C. Electromagnetic wave
11. B. Energy cannot be created or destroyed, only transformed.
12. B. Resonance
13. B. Atom
14. C. Max Planck
15. C. 9.8 m/s^2

More Fun Facts About Physics

1. The Earth's magnetic field is not fixed; it flips every few hundred thousand years, with the north and south poles reversing positions.
2. At the quantum level, particles can exist in multiple states at once, a phenomenon known as superposition.
3. Lasers are so precise that they can be used to cut through diamonds or perform delicate eye surgery.

4. Time dilation, a concept in Einstein's theory of relativity, means time passes more slowly in stronger gravitational fields or for objects moving closer to the speed of light.
5. A teaspoon of matter from a neutron star would weigh as much as Mount Everest.
6. The Doppler effect explains why the sound of a passing car changes pitch as it moves toward and then away from you.
7. Space itself is expanding, causing galaxies to move farther apart over time, a discovery attributed to Edwin Hubble.
8. Water is densest at 4°C, which is why ice floats on liquid water, creating an insulating layer that helps aquatic life survive in freezing temperatures.
9. If you could travel at the speed of light, you would experience time standing still.
10. The Heisenberg Uncertainty Principle states that you cannot precisely measure both the position and momentum of a particle at the same time.

Trivia Quiz Part 2: Physics

1. **What is the term for the energy an object has due to its motion?**
   A. Potential energy
   B. Kinetic energy
   C. Thermal energy
   D. Chemical energy
2. **What is the name of the device used to measure electric current?**
   A. Voltmeter
   B. Ammeter
   C. Ohmmeter
   D. Barometer
3. **True or False: Black holes can emit light.**
4. **Which law states that every action has an equal and opposite reaction?**
   A. First law of thermodynamics
   B. Newton's First Law
   C. Newton's Third Law
   D. Hooke's Law
5. **What is the term for the point where light rays converge after passing through a lens?**
   A. Focus
   B. Aperture
   C. Focal point
   D. Diffraction point
6. **What is the name of the force that holds protons and neutrons together in an atomic nucleus?**
   A. Electromagnetic force
   B. Gravitational force
   C. Strong nuclear force
   D. Weak nuclear force

7. **What is the name of the boundary around a black hole beyond which nothing can escape?**
   A. Event horizon
   B. Singularity
   C. Schwarzschild radius
   D. Cosmic horizon
8. **What is the SI unit of electrical resistance?**
   A. Volt
   B. Ampere
   C. Ohm
   D. Watt
9. **What phenomenon causes a red shift in the light of distant galaxies?**
   A. Gravitational lensing
   B. Expanding universe
   C. Doppler effect
   D. Cosmic microwave background
10. **What is the temperature at which molecular motion theoretically stops?**
    A. 0 Kelvin
    B. 0 Celsius
    C. 0 Fahrenheit
    D. 273 Kelvin
11. **What particle is responsible for carrying the force of electromagnetism?**
    A. Photon
    B. Electron
    C. Proton
    D. Neutron
12. **Who formulated the principle of buoyancy?**
    A. Archimedes
    B. Galileo
    C. Pascal
    D. Bernoulli

13. **What type of particle is exchanged in a nuclear fusion reaction in the Sun?**
    A. Neutrino
    B. Proton
    C. Electron
    D. Positron
14. **What is the term for the bending of a wave as it passes through a medium?**
    A. Reflection
    B. Refraction
    C. Diffraction
    D. Interference
15. **What is the theory that describes the fundamental forces and particles of the universe?**
    A. Theory of Relativity
    B. String Theory
    C. Standard Model
    D. Big Bang Theory

Answers Part 2: Physics

1. B. Kinetic energy
2. B. Ammeter
3. False (Black holes themselves don't emit light, but their accretion disks can.)
4. C. Newton's Third Law
5. C. Focal point
6. C. Strong nuclear force
7. A. Event horizon
8. C. Ohm
9. B. Expanding universe
10. A. 0 Kelvin
11. A. Photon
12. A. Archimedes
13. A. Neutrino
14. B. Refraction
15. C. Standard Model

Chapter 5: Chemistry

Fun Facts About Chemistry

1. Diamonds and graphite are both made of carbon, but their atoms are arranged differently, which gives them vastly different properties.
2. Helium is the only element that doesn't solidify under normal pressure—it remains a liquid even at absolute zero unless compressed.
3. Water is the only substance that expands when it freezes, making ice less dense than liquid water, which is why it floats.
4. The most abundant element in the human body is oxygen, accounting for about 65% of body mass.
5. The element gallium melts in your hand because it has a melting point of only 29.76°C (85.57°F).
6. Pure gold is so soft that it can be moulded by hand, and a single gram can be stretched into a sheet covering a square meter.
7. The "smell" of rain comes from a compound called geosmin, which is produced by soil-dwelling bacteria.
8. Hydrogen, the lightest and most abundant element, makes up about 75% of the universe by mass.
9. The first man-made element was technetium, created in 1937 by bombarding molybdenum atoms with deuterons.
10. Table salt (sodium chloride) is made of two elements that are highly reactive and toxic on their own but safe when combined.

Trivia Quiz Part 1: Chemistry

1. **What is the most abundant element in the Earth's crust?**
   A. Silicon
   B. Oxygen
   C. Iron
   D. Aluminium
2. **What is the chemical formula for water?**
   A. H2O
   B. O2H
   C. OH2
   D. HO
3. **Which gas is known as the "laughing gas"?**
   A. Nitrogen
   B. Nitrous oxide
   C. Carbon dioxide
   D. Helium
4. **True or False: All acids are harmful to humans.**
5. **What is the pH of a neutral solution?**
   A. 0
   B. 7
   C. 10
   D. 14
6. **What is the heaviest naturally occurring element on Earth?**
   A. Uranium
   B. Plutonium
   C. Lead
   D. Gold

7. **Which scientist is credited with creating the first periodic table?**
   A. John Dalton
   B. Dmitri Mendeleev
   C. Marie Curie
   D. Ernest Rutherford

8. **What is the name of the process by which plants convert carbon dioxide and water into glucose and oxygen?**
   A. Respiration
   B. Photosynthesis
   C. Fermentation
   D. Oxidation

9. **What is the SI unit for measuring the amount of a substance?**
   A. Mole
   B. Gram
   C. Liter
   D. Joule

10. **What type of bond involves the sharing of electron pairs between atoms?**
    A. Ionic bond
    B. Covalent bond
    C. Metallic bond
    D. Hydrogen bond

11. **What element has the chemical symbol 'K'?**
    A. Krypton
    B. Potassium
    C. Calcium
    D. Copper

12. **Which acid is commonly found in car batteries?**
    A. Hydrochloric acid
    B. Sulfuric acid
    C. Acetic acid
    D. Nitric acid
13. **What is the term for the amount of energy required to remove an electron from an atom?**
    A. Electronegativity
    B. Ionisation energy
    C. Electron affinity
    D. Atomic mass
14. **What type of reaction releases energy in the form of heat or light?**
    A. Endothermic reaction
    B. Exothermic reaction
    C. Neutralisation reaction
    D. Precipitation reaction
15. **What is the primary component of natural gas?**
    A. Methane
    B. Propane
    C. Ethane
    D. Butane

Answers Part 1: Chemistry

1. **B. Oxygen**
2. **A. H2O**
3. **B. Nitrous oxide**
4. **False** (Not all acids are harmful; some, like citric acid, are found in food.)
5. **B. 7**
6. **A. Uranium**
7. **B. Dmitri Mendeleev**
8. **B. Photosynthesis**
9. **A. Mole**
10. **B. Covalent bond**
11. **B. Potassium**
12. **B. Sulfuric acid**
13. **B. Ionisation energy**
14. **B. Exothermic reaction**
15. **A. Methane**

More Fun Facts About Chemistry

1. The human body contains about 0.2 milligrams of gold, most of it in the bloodstream.
2. Mercury is the only metal that is liquid at room temperature, while gallium can melt in your hand.
3. The element bromine is a liquid at room temperature, making it one of only two elements (the other is mercury) in this state.
4. Soap works because it has molecules with two ends: one that is attracted to water and one that repels it, allowing it to dissolve grease and dirt.

5. Table sugar (sucrose) is made of two simple sugars: glucose and fructose.
6. The chemical element with the highest melting point is tungsten, at 3,422°C (6,192°F).
7. Liquid nitrogen boils at -196°C (-321°F) and is commonly used for freezing food or conducting experiments.
8. The fizz in soda comes from carbon dioxide gas dissolved under pressure, which forms bubbles when the pressure is released.
9. The discovery of the element radium by Marie and Pierre Curie in 1898 paved the way for the development of X-ray machines.
10. The rarest naturally occurring element on Earth is astatine, with less than 1 gram present in the Earth's crust at any time.

Trivia Quiz Part 2: Chemistry

1. **What is the most reactive group of elements in the periodic table?**
   A. Noble gases
   B. Alkali metals
   C. Halogens
   D. Transition metals
2. **What is the chemical formula for table salt?**
   A. NaCl
   B. KCl
   C. MgCl2
   D. CaCl2

3. **Which element is commonly used in balloons and airships?**
    A. Hydrogen
    B. Helium
    C. Nitrogen
    D. Oxygen
4. **True or False: The pH scale ranges from 0 to 14.**
5. **What is the name of the bond formed between oppositely charged ions?**
    A. Covalent bond
    B. Ionic bond
    C. Metallic bond
    D. Hydrogen bond
6. **Which element is a key component in steel?**
    A. Aluminium
    B. Iron
    C. Copper
    D. Zinc
7. **What is the name of the process in which a liquid changes into a gas?**
    A. Sublimation
    B. Condensation
    C. Vaporisation
    D. Precipitation
8. **What is the lightest element in the periodic table?**
    A. Hydrogen
    B. Helium
    C. Lithium
    D. Oxygen

9. **Which acid is found in vinegar?**
   A. Sulfuric acid
   B. Acetic acid
   C. Citric acid
   D. Hydrochloric acid
10. **What is the chemical symbol for silver?**
    A. Si
    B. Ag
    C. Au
    D. Al
11. **What is the term for a substance that speeds up a chemical reaction without being consumed?**
    A. Solvent
    B. Catalyst
    C. Reactant
    D. Inhibitor
12. **What element has the atomic number 6?**
    A. Carbon
    B. Nitrogen
    C. Oxygen
    D. Boron
13. **What type of reaction occurs when two substances combine to form one compound?**
    A. Decomposition reaction
    B. Synthesis reaction
    C. Combustion reaction
    D. Neutralisation reaction

14. What is the name of the process that separates a liquid into its individual components using boiling points?
    A. Filtration
    B. Distillation
    C. Chromatography
    D. Precipitation
15. What colour does copper turn when it oxidises?
    A. Green
    B. Blue
    C. Black
    D. White

Answers Part 2: Chemistry

1. B. Alkali metals
2. A. NaCl
3. B. Helium
4. True
5. B. Ionic bond
6. B. Iron
7. C. Vaporisation
8. A. Hydrogen
9. B. Acetic acid
10. B. Ag
11. B. Catalyst
12. A. Carbon
13. B. Synthesis reaction
14. B. Distillation
15. A. Green

Chapter 6: Sports

Fun Facts About Sports

1. The Olympic Games were first held in 776 BCE in Olympia, Greece, and featured only one event: a footrace.
2. Basketball was invented in 1891 by James Naismith, who used a soccer ball and two peach baskets as goals.
3. Cricket is believed to have originated in England during the 16th century and is now one of the most popular sports globally.
4. The FIFA World Cup is the most-watched sporting event in the world, with over 3.5 billion people tuning in for the 2018 tournament.
5. The fastest recorded tennis serve was by Sam Groth, clocking in at 263 km/h (163.7 mph) in 2012.
6. Michael Phelps, the most decorated Olympian of all time, has won 28 medals, 23 of them gold.
7. The longest marathon in history lasted 65 days, with a baseball game held in Illinois, USA, in 1981.
8. Golf balls have dimples to reduce air resistance and allow them to fly farther.
9. Formula One cars can accelerate from 0 to 100 mph and back to 0 in just 4 seconds.
10. The Boston Marathon is the world's oldest annual marathon, first held in 1897.

Trivia Quiz Part 1: Sports

1. **Which country has won the most FIFA World Cups?**
   A. Germany
   B. Brazil
   C. Italy
   D. Argentina
2. **What sport is known as the "king of sports"?**
   A. Basketball
   B. Cricket
   C. Soccer (Football)
   D. Tennis
3. **Which athlete is known as the "Fastest Man on Earth"?**
   A. Carl Lewis
   B. Usain Bolt
   C. Michael Johnson
   D. Jesse Owens
4. **True or False: The first modern Olympics were held in Athens, Greece, in 1896.**
5. **What is the term for scoring three goals in a single game in soccer?**
   A. Hattrick
   B. Triple Crown
   C. Three-peat
   D. Goal streak
6. **Which team holds the record for the most NBA championships?**
   A. Chicago Bulls
   B. Los Angeles Lakers
   C. Boston Celtics
   D. Golden State Warriors

7. **What is the name of the trophy awarded to the winner of the NHL playoffs?**
   A. Stanley Cup
   B. Super Bowl Trophy
   C. Grey Cup
   D. Claret Jug

8. **Which female tennis player has won the most Grand Slam singles titles?**
   A. Steffi Graf
   B. Serena Williams
   C. Margaret Court
   D. Martina Navratilova

9. **What is the national sport of Japan?**
   A. Sumo Wrestling
   B. Baseball
   C. Judo
   D. Karate

10. **How many players are there on a rugby union team?**
    A. 11
    B. 13
    C. 15
    D. 18

11. **What is the highest possible score in a single game of 10-pin bowling?**
    A. 200
    B. 250
    C. 300
    D. 350

12. **Which country has hosted the Summer Olympics the most times?**
    A. United States
    B. United Kingdom
    C. France
    D. Japan
13. **What is the name of the annual bike race held in France?**
    A. Giro d'Italia
    B. Tour de France
    C. Paris-Roubaix
    D. La Vuelta
14. **What sport is played at Wimbledon?**
    A. Golf
    B. Cricket
    C. Tennis
    D. Rugby
15. **Who holds the record for the most home runs in Major League Baseball?**
    A. Babe Ruth
    B. Barry Bonds
    C. Hank Aaron
    D. Alex Rodriguez

Answers Part 1: Sports

1. B. Brazil
2. C. Soccer (Football)
3. B. Usain Bolt
4. True
5. A. Hattrick
6. C. Boston Celtics
7. A. Stanley Cup
8. C. Margaret Court
9. A. Sumo Wrestling
10. C. 15
11. C. 300
12. A. United States
13. B. Tour de France
14. C. Tennis
15. B. Barry Bonds

More Fun Facts About Sports

1. In baseball, a "perfect game" occurs when a pitcher allows no opposing players to reach base during the entire game. Only 24 such games have been recorded in Major League Baseball history.
2. The highest-scoring basketball game in NBA history occurred in 1983, when the Detroit Pistons defeated the Denver Nuggets 186–184 after triple overtime.

3. In 1969, a soccer match between El Salvador and Honduras sparked a brief war, known as the "Football War."
4. Wimbledon, the world's oldest tennis tournament, began in 1877 and has been played on grass ever since.
5. The longest tennis match in history lasted 11 hours and 5 minutes, played between John Isner and Nicolas Mahut at Wimbledon in 2010.
6. The Tour de France covers approximately 3,500 kilometres (2,200 miles) over three weeks, making it one of the most gruelling athletic events.
7. The Olympic torch is lit in Greece and travels around the world before arriving at the host city for the Games.
8. The Chicago Cubs broke a 108-year drought by winning the 2016 World Series, the longest championship drought in major professional sports history.
9. Cricket matches can last anywhere from a few hours (T20 format) to five days (Test matches).
10. In golf, the term "birdie" means scoring one stroke under par on a hole, while an "albatross" means scoring three strokes under par.

Trivia Quiz Part 2: Sports

1. **Who holds the record for the most goals scored in a single FIFA World Cup?**
    A. Pele
    B. Miroslav Klose
    C. Just Fontaine
    D. Cristiano Ronaldo
2. **Which country hosted the first Rugby World Cup in 1987?**
    A. Australia
    B. England
    C. New Zealand
    D. South Africa
3. **What is the name of the award given annually to the NFL's most valuable player?**
    A. Heisman Trophy
    B. Vince Lombardi Award
    C. MVP Award
    D. Walter Payton Award
4. **True or False: A marathon is exactly 26.2 miles long.**
5. **What is the term for a strikeout in baseball where the batter doesn't swing at the third strike?**
    A. Called strike
    B. Caught looking
    C. Dropped third strike
    D. Foul tip

6. What is the nickname of Muhammad Ali, widely regarded as the greatest boxer of all time?
   A. The Champ
   B. The Greatest
   C. The King
   D. The Legend
7. Which country has won the most medals in the history of the Summer Olympics?
   A. China
   B. United States
   C. Russia
   D. Germany
8. What is the standard length of a soccer field used in international matches?
   A. 90–120 meters
   B. 80–100 meters
   C. 100–110 meters
   D. 110–130 meters
9. What is the name of the prestigious golf tournament held annually at Augusta National Golf Club?
   A. The Open Championship
   B. The Masters
   C. The PGA Championship
   D. The Ryder Cup
10. Which athlete lit the Olympic cauldron at the 1996 Atlanta Games?
    A. Carl Lewis
    B. Michael Johnson
    C. Muhammad Ali
    D. Jesse Owens

11. **What is the maximum score in a game of darts using three darts?**
    A. 150
    B. 180
    C. 200
    D. 300
12. **Which country's national team is nicknamed the "All Blacks"?**
    A. Australia
    B. New Zealand
    C. South Africa
    D. England
13. **What is the term for the part of a baseball field outside the bases?**
    A. Infield
    B. Outfield
    C. Dugout
    D. Bullpen
14. **Who was the first athlete to win gold medals in five consecutive Olympic Games?**
    A. Usain Bolt
    B. Carl Lewis
    C. Michael Phelps
    D. Al Oerter
15. **Which sport features a move called the "double axel"?**
    A. Gymnastics
    B. Figure skating
    C. Diving
    D. Pole vault

Answers Part 2: Sports

1. C. Just Fontaine
2. C. New Zealand
3. C. MVP Award
4. True
5. B. Caught looking
6. B. The Greatest
7. B. United States
8. D. 110–130 meters
9. B. The Masters
10. C. Muhammad Ali
11. B. 180
12. B. New Zealand
13. B. Outfield
14. D. Al Oerter
15. B. Figure skating

Chapter 7: Soccer

Fun Facts About Soccer

1. Soccer, known as "football", outside North America, is the most popular sport in the world, with over 4 billion fans globally.
2. The oldest soccer club in the world is Sheffield FC, founded in 1857 in England.
3. The fastest goal in soccer history was scored just 2.8 seconds into the game by Nawaf Al-Abed in a Saudi league match in 2009.
4. Pelé, widely regarded as one of the greatest players of all time, scored over 1,280 goals during his career.
5. The FIFA World Cup trophy is made of 18-carat gold and weighs about 6 kilograms.
6. Lionel Messi holds the record for the most goals scored in a calendar year, with 91 goals in 2012.
7. The largest soccer stadium in the world is Rungrado 1st of May Stadium in North Korea, with a seating capacity of 114,000.
8. The first Women's World Cup was held in 1991 in China, and the United States won the inaugural tournament.
9. Goalkeepers were not allowed to wear gloves in official matches until the 1970s.
10. Cristiano Ronaldo is the first player in history to score in five consecutive FIFA World Cups (2006–2022).

Trivia Quiz Part 1: Soccer

1. **Which country has won the most FIFA World Cups?**
   A. Germany
   B. Brazil
   C. Italy
   D. Argentina
2. **Who holds the record for the most goals scored in a single World Cup tournament?**
   A. Pelé
   B. Miroslav Klose
   C. Just Fontaine
   D. Ronaldo
3. **True or False: The Premier League was founded in 1992.**
4. **What is the name of the prestigious European club competition organised by UEFA?**
   A. Europa League
   B. Champions League
   C. Conference League
   D. Cup Winners' Cup
5. **Which player is known as "The King of Soccer"?**
   A. Diego Maradona
   B. Cristiano Ronaldo
   C. Lionel Messi
   D. Pelé
6. **What is the standard size of a soccer goal?**
   A. 6.5m x 2.1m
   B. 7.32m x 2.44m
   C. 8m x 3m
   D. 7.5m x 2.5m

7. **Which country hosted the first FIFA World Cup in 1930?**
    A. Uruguay
    B. Argentina
    C. Brazil
    D. Italy
8. **Which English soccer club is nicknamed "The Red Devils"?**
    A. Arsenal
    B. Liverpool
    C. Manchester United
    D. Chelsea
9. **Who is the all-time top scorer in the history of the Champions League?**
    A. Lionel Messi
    B. Cristiano Ronaldo
    C. Robert Lewandowski
    D. Karim Benzema
10. **Which country won the 2010 FIFA World Cup?**
    A. Spain
    B. Netherlands
    C. Germany
    D. Brazil
11. **What is the term for a player scoring three goals in a single game?**
    A. Brace
    B. Hat-trick
    C. Triple crown
    D. Trifecta

12. What is the name of the trophy awarded to the
winner of the Premier League?
A. Premier Cup
B. FA Trophy
C. Premier League Trophy
D. Community Shield
13. What is the maximum duration of extra time in
a standard soccer match?
A. 15 minutes
B. 20 minutes
C. 30 minutes
D. 40 minutes
14. Which country is home to the El Clasico
rivalry between Real Madrid and Barcelona?
A. Italy
B. Spain
C. Portugal
D. Argentina
15. Who won the Ballon d'Or in 2023?
A. Lionel Messi
B. Erling Haaland
C. Kylian Mbappé
D. Cristiano Ronaldo

Answers Part 1: Soccer

1. B. Brazil
2. C. Just Fontaine
3. True
4. B. Champions League
5. D. Pelé
6. B. 7.32m x 2.44m
7. A. Uruguay
8. C. Manchester United
9. B. Cristiano Ronaldo
10. A. Spain
11. B. Hat-trick
12. C. Premier League Trophy
13. C. 30 minutes
14. B. Spain
15. A. Lionel Messi

Chapter 8: Cricket

Fun Facts About Cricket

1. Cricket is one of the oldest sports in the world, with records of it being played as early as the 16th century in England.
2. The longest cricket match in history was between England and South Africa in 1939 and lasted 12 days—it ended in a draw because the English team had to catch their ship back home.
3. The Ashes, a famous Test series between England and Australia, began in 1882 when England lost to Australia at The Oval, sparking a satirical obituary declaring the death of English cricket.
4. Sachin Tendulkar, widely regarded as one of the greatest cricketers of all time, is the only player to have scored 100 international centuries.
5. Chris Gayle holds the record for the fastest century in T20 cricket, taking just 30 balls while playing for the Royal Challengers Bangalore in the IPL.
6. The first-ever Cricket World Cup was held in 1975, and the West Indies emerged as champions.
7. Cricket is the second-most-watched sport globally, with over 2.5 billion fans.
8. The heaviest cricket bat ever used in a match weighed 4.4 kilograms and was wielded by West Indies cricketer Clive Lloyd.
9. Muttiah Muralitharan of Sri Lanka holds the record for the most Test wickets, with 800 dismissals.

10. Cricket is played professionally in over 100 countries, with India being home to the largest fan base.

Trivia Quiz Part 1: Cricket

1. **Which country has won the most ICC Cricket World Cups?**
   A. India
   B. Australia
   C. West Indies
   D. England
2. **Who is known as the "God of Cricket"?**
   A. Virat Kohli
   B. Don Bradman
   C. Sachin Tendulkar
   D. Jacques Kallis
3. **True or False: A Test match lasts for a maximum of five days.**
4. **What is the term for dismissing a batsman without scoring any runs?**
   A. Duck
   B. Maiden
   C. Golden run
   D. Goose
5. **Which bowler has taken the most wickets in Test cricket?**
   A. Shane Warne
   B. Muttiah Muralitharan
   C. Anil Kumble
   D. James Anderson

6. **What is the name of the cricket stadium in Melbourne that hosts the Boxing Day Test?**
   A. Adelaide Oval
   B. Sydney Cricket Ground
   C. Melbourne Cricket Ground
   D. Gabba
7. **Who was the first cricketer to score a double century in a One Day International (ODI)?**
   A. Chris Gayle
   B. Virender Sehwag
   C. Rohit Sharma
   D. Sachin Tendulkar
8. **What is the length of the pitch in a cricket field?**
   A. 18 yards
   B. 20 yards
   C. 22 yards
   D. 24 yards
9. **Which cricketing nation is nicknamed the "Proteas"?**
   A. South Africa
   B. New Zealand
   C. Sri Lanka
   D. Pakistan
10. **What is the maximum number of overs in a T20 cricket match?**
    A. 10
    B. 20
    C. 30
    D. 40

11. **Who captained India to their first Cricket World Cup victory in 1983?**
    A. MS Dhoni
    B. Kapil Dev
    C. Sunil Gavaskar
    D. Ravi Shastri
12. **What is the name of the league that revolutionised cricket with its short format and big entertainment value?**
    A. Big Bash League
    B. Indian Premier League (IPL)
    C. Caribbean Premier League
    D. Pakistan Super League
13. **Who is the only bowler to take all 10 wickets in a single Test innings?**
    A. Anil Kumble
    B. Jim Laker
    C. Shane Warne
    D. Both A and B
14. **What is the term for a bowler delivering six balls in a row in cricket?**
    A. Maiden
    B. Over
    C. Spell
    D. Innings
15. **What is the name of the annual cricket series between England and Australia?**
    A. Border-Gavaskar Trophy
    B. The Ashes
    C. Frank Worrell Trophy
    D. Pataudi Trophy

Answers Part 1: Cricket Trivia

1. B. Australia
2. C. Sachin Tendulkar
3. True
4. A. Duck
5. B. Muttiah Muralitharan
6. C. Melbourne Cricket Ground
7. D. Sachin Tendulkar
8. C. 22 yards
9. A. South Africa
10. D. 40 (20 overs per team)
11. B. Kapil Dev
12. B. Indian Premier League (IPL)
13. D. Both A and B (Anil Kumble and Jim Laker)
14. B. Over
15. B. The Ashes

Chapter 9: Rugby League

Fun Facts About Rugby League

1. Rugby league was formed in 1895 when 22 clubs in Northern England broke away from rugby union over the issue of player payments, creating the Northern Rugby Football Union.
2. The Rugby League World Cup is one of the oldest international sports tournaments, first held in 1954 in France.
3. The St. George Dragons hold the record for the most consecutive premierships in Australian rugby league, winning 11 titles in a row from 1956 to 1966.
4. The "Golden Boot Award" is given annually to the best rugby league player in the world.
5. Rugby league matches are played with 13 players per team on the field, compared to 15 in rugby union.
6. The State of Origin series between Queensland and New South Wales is considered one of the fiercest rivalries in rugby league, drawing millions of viewers annually.
7. Rugby league was the first sport to introduce the concept of a video referee, with its first use in 1996.
8. The record for the most points scored in a single rugby league match is held by Dave Brown of the Eastern Suburbs, who scored 45 points in 1935.
9. The Super League, launched in 1996, revolutionised rugby league in Europe with a summer season format.

10. Rugby league is most popular in countries like Australia, England, New Zealand, and Papua New Guinea, where it is the national sport.

Trivia Quiz Part 1: Rugby League

1. **Which country has won the most Rugby League World Cups?**
   A. England
   B. Australia
   C. New Zealand
   D. France

2. **What is the maximum number of tackles a team is allowed before they must hand over possession?**
   A. 4
   B. 5
   C. 6
   D. 7

3. **True or False: A try in rugby league is worth 5 points.**

4. **Which team has won the most NRL Premierships?**
   A. Sydney Roosters
   B. Melbourne Storm
   C. South Sydney Rabbitohs
   D. Brisbane Broncos

5. **What is the name of the annual rugby league competition in England?**
   A. Premiership Rugby
   B. Super League
   C. Gallagher League
   D. Championship
6. **Who holds the record for the most tries scored in rugby league history?**
   A. Billy Slater
   B. Brian Bevan
   C. Greg Inglis
   D. Jarryd Hayne
7. **What is the term for a kick that aims to restart play after a try has been scored?**
   A. Drop kick
   B. Conversion
   C. Penalty kick
   D. Scrum
8. **Which country hosted the first Rugby League World Cup?**
   A. England
   B. France
   C. Australia
   D. New Zealand
9. **How many players are on the field for each rugby league team during a game?**
   A. 13
   B. 14
   C. 15
   D. 12

10. **What is the name of the famous rugby league series played between Queensland and New South Wales?**
    A. Origin Cup
    B. State of Origin
    C. Australian Series
    D. National Derby

11. **What is the standard length of a rugby league field?**
    A. 90 meters
    B. 100 meters
    C. 120 meters
    D. 140 meters

12. **Who is the youngest player to ever play in a Rugby League World Cup final?**
    A. Ellery Hanley
    B. Brad Fittler
    C. James Tedesco
    D. Sam Tomkins

13. **What is the term for the defensive line of players in rugby league?**
    A. Forward pack
    B. Defensive wall
    C. Ruck
    D. Line defence

14. **Which team won the inaugural Super League Grand Final in 1998?**
    A. Wigan Warriors
    B. Leeds Rhinos
    C. Bradford Bulls
    D. St. Helens

15. **What is the term for a penalty kick that goes through the posts in rugby league?**
    A. Drop goal
    B. Field goal
    C. Penalty goal
    D. Conversion

Answers Part 1: Rugby League

1. B. Australia
2. C. 6
3. False (A try is worth 4 points.)
4. C. South Sydney Rabbitohs
5. B. Super League
6. B. Brian Bevan
7. B. Conversion
8. B. France
9. A. 13
10. B. State of Origin
11. C. 120 meters
12. B. Brad Fittler
13. D. Line defence
14. C. Bradford Bulls
15. C. Penalty goal

Chapter 10: Rugby Union

Fun Facts About Rugby Union

1. Rugby union originated in 1823 at Rugby School in England when William Webb Ellis reportedly picked up the ball and ran with it during a football (soccer) game.
2. The Rugby World Cup trophy is named the *William Webb Ellis Cup* in honour of the sport's supposed founder.
3. Rugby union is played with 15 players per side on the field, compared to 13 in rugby league.
4. New Zealand's All Blacks perform the *haka*, a traditional Maori war dance, before each match, intimidating their opponents.
5. The first-ever Rugby World Cup was held in 1987 and was jointly hosted by New Zealand and Australia, with New Zealand emerging as the champions.
6. The Calcutta Cup, contested between England and Scotland, is the oldest international rugby trophy, first awarded in 1879.
7. The longest rugby union match lasted over 30 hours and was played in England in 2011 to raise money for charity.
8. South Africa has won the most Rugby World Cup titles, with four victories (1995, 2007, 2019, 2023).
9. Rugby union is played in over 120 countries, with teams competing in regional and global tournaments, including the Six Nations and Rugby Championship.

10. The fastest try in international rugby union was scored by Lee Jones of Scotland, just seven seconds into a match in 2013.

Trivia Quiz Part 1: Rugby Union

1. **Which team has won the most Rugby World Cup titles?**
   A. England
   B. South Africa
   C. New Zealand
   D. Australia
2. **How many points is a try worth in rugby union?**
   A. 3
   B. 4
   C. 5
   D. 7
3. **True or False: Rugby union matches are 90 minutes long.**
4. **What is the term for the line of players who compete to catch the ball thrown in during a lineout?**
   A. Scrum line
   B. Lineout jumpers
   C. Forwards
   D. Backs

5. Which competition is contested annually
    between England, Ireland, Scotland, Wales,
    France, and Italy?
    A. Rugby Championship
    B. Six Nations
    C. British & Irish Lions Tour
    D. Tri-Nations
6. Who is the all-time top points scorer in
    international rugby union?
    A. Dan Carter
    B. Jonny Wilkinson
    C. Owen Farrell
    D. Richie McCaw
7. What is the maximum number of substitutes
    allowed in a rugby union match?
    A. 5
    B. 7
    C. 8
    D. 10
8. What is the name of the position responsible
    for throwing the ball during a lineout?
    A. Prop
    B. Hooker
    C. Scrum-half
    D. Lock
9. What is the standard length of a rugby union
    field?
    A. 90 meters
    B. 100 meters
    C. 120 meters
    D. 150 meters

10. **Which country won the 2003 Rugby World Cup?**
    A. England
    B. New Zealand
    C. Australia
    D. South Africa
11. **What is the name of the tour where a combined team from England, Ireland, Scotland, and Wales competes against Southern Hemisphere nations?**
    A. Barbarians Tour
    B. Lions Tour
    C. Pacific Nations Tour
    D. All Blacks Challenge
12. **What is the term for scoring a try, conversion, penalty, and drop goal in a single match?**
    A. Hat-trick
    B. Grand Slam
    C. Full House
    D. Triple Crown
13. **Which rugby union team is nicknamed the "Wallabies"?**
    A. New Zealand
    B. South Africa
    C. England
    D. Australia
14. **What is the name of the trophy awarded to the winner of the Rugby World Cup?**
    A. Ellis Cup
    B. Rugby Championship Trophy
    C. William Webb Ellis Cup
    D. World Rugby Shield

15. **Who is the youngest player to have appeared in a Rugby World Cup final?**
    A. Jonah Lomu
    B. George North
    C. Cheslin Kolbe
    D. Matt Giteau

Answers Part 1: Rugby Union

1. B. South Africa
2. C. 5
3. False (Matches are 80 minutes long.)
4. B. Lineout jumpers
5. B. Six Nations
6. A. Dan Carter
7. C. 8
8. B. Hooker
9. C. 120 meters
10. A. England
11. B. Lions Tour
12. C. Full House
13. D. Australia
14. C. William Webb Ellis Cup
15. A. Jonah Lomu

Chapter 11: Darts

Fun Facts About Darts

1. Darts originated as a training game for archers in medieval England, using the end of a barrel as a target.
2. The standard dartboard layout, called the "London Board" or "Clock Board," was first created in 1896.
3. The highest score a player can achieve in a single turn (three darts) is 180, known as a "maximum."
4. The bullseye on a dartboard is worth 50 points, while the outer bull is worth 25 points.
5. The sport's governing body, the Professional Darts Corporation (PDC), organises the most prestigious tournaments, including the World Darts Championship.
6. Phil "The Power" Taylor is considered the greatest darts player of all time, with 16 World Championship titles to his name.
7. In 2009, the first televised nine-dart finish (the perfect leg) was achieved by John Lowe. It involves hitting 501 points in just nine darts.
8. The game of darts is so precise that professional players can often hit the same target area within millimetres repeatedly.
9. Darts was once banned in pubs in the 1900s because it was considered a game of chance until it was proven in court to be a game of skill.
10. Modern dartboards are made from sisal fibres, which allow the darts to penetrate and then self-heal after removal.

Trivia Quiz Part 1: Darts

1. **What is the highest possible score in a single round of darts (three darts)?**
   A. 150
   B. 160
   C. 180
   D. 190
2. **What is the term for scoring zero points in a round of darts?**
   A. Double
   B. Bust
   C. Miss
   D. Null
3. **True or False: The outer bullseye is worth more points than the inner bullseye.**
4. **What is the name of the most prestigious darts tournament in the world?**
   A. Grand Slam of Darts
   B. World Darts Championship
   C. Premier League Darts
   D. UK Open
5. **Which country is considered the birthplace of modern darts?**
   A. Scotland
   B. Wales
   C. England
   D. Ireland
6. **What is the standard starting score in a game of 501?**
   A. 501
   B. 300
   C. 180
   D. 750

7. **Who is the most decorated darts player in history?**
   A. Michael van Gerwen
   B. Phil Taylor
   C. Raymond van Barneveld
   D. Gary Anderson

8. **What is the term for finishing a leg of darts with three perfect throws (nine darts)?**
   A. Double finish
   B. Triple top
   C. Nine-dart finish
   D. Maximum leg

9. **How many points is the triple 20 worth?**
   A. 40
   B. 50
   C. 60
   D. 80

10. **What is the circumference of a standard dartboard?**
    A. 34 inches
    B. 36 inches
    C. 38 inches
    D. 40 inches

11. **What is the material most commonly used for modern dartboard construction?**
    A. Cork
    B. Plastic
    C. Sisal
    D. Wood

12. **Who was the first player to achieve a televised nine-dart finish?**
    A. Eric Bristow
    B. John Lowe
    C. Jocky Wilson
    D. Phil Taylor
13. **Which score must a player hit to win a leg in a game of 501?**
    A. 0
    B. 1
    C. 50
    D. 25
14. **What is the name of the tournament that features only the top players in the world and is held annually at Alexandra Palace?**
    A. World Grand Prix
    B. Premier League Darts
    C. World Matchplay
    D. PDC World Darts Championship
15. **Which player is nicknamed "The Flying Scotsman"?**
    A. Peter Wright
    B. Gary Anderson
    C. Jocky Wilson
    D. Alan Warriner-Little

Answers Part 1: Darts Trivia

1. **C. 180**
2. **B. Bust**
3. **False** (The inner bullseye is worth more: 50 points.)
4. **B. World Darts Championship**
5. **C. England**
6. **A. 501**
7. **B. Phil Taylor**
8. **C. Nine-dart finish**
9. **C. 60**
10. **B. 36 inches**
11. **C. Sisal**
12. **B. John Lowe**
13. **A. 0**
14. **D. PDC World Darts Championship**
15. **B. Gary Anderson**

Chapter 12: Golf

Fun Facts About Golf

1. Golf originated in Scotland in the 15th century, and the Old Course at St. Andrews is widely regarded as the birthplace of the game.
2. The modern golf ball has 336 dimples on average, which help it travel farther and straighter.
3. Tiger Woods was just 21 years old when he won his first Masters Tournament in 1997, becoming the youngest champion in history.
4. The term "birdie" originated in the United States in the early 1900s and means scoring one stroke under par on a hole.
5. The longest recorded drive in professional golf is 515 yards, achieved by Mike Austin in 1974.
6. The average golf hole is designed to be completed in about 4 strokes, but par-3, par-4, and par-5 holes offer varying challenges.
7. The Ryder Cup, a biennial competition between Europe and the United States, began in 1927.
8. Phil Mickelson is the oldest golfer to win a major championship, capturing the PGA Championship at the age of 50 in 2021.
9. Golf was reintroduced to the Olympics in 2016 after being absent for 112 years.
10. The shortest hole in professional golf is the 8th hole at the TPC Sawgrass Stadium Course, measuring just 137 yards.

Trivia Quiz Part 1: Golf

1. **What is the term for completing a hole one stroke under par?**
   A. Eagle
   B. Birdie
   C. Par
   D. Bogey
2. **Which golfer has won the most major championships?**
   A. Tiger Woods
   B. Jack Nicklaus
   C. Arnold Palmer
   D. Phil Mickelson
3. **True or False: A standard round of golf consists of 18 holes.**
4. **What is the term for a score of three strokes under par on a single hole?**
   A. Birdie
   B. Double Eagle (Albatross)
   C. Bogey
   D. Hole-in-one
5. **What is the name of the most prestigious golf tournament held annually at Augusta National Golf Club?**
   A. The Masters
   B. The Open Championship
   C. PGA Championship
   D. U.S. Open
6. **Which country is credited with inventing golf?**
   A. England
   B. Ireland
   C. Scotland
   D. United States

7. **What colour jacket is awarded to the winner of The Masters?**
   A. Red
   B. Green
   C. Blue
   D. Gold

8. **Who holds the record for the lowest score in a single round at a major championship?**
   A. Rory McIlroy
   B. Branden Grace
   C. Dustin Johnson
   D. Greg Norman

9. **What is the standard number of clubs allowed in a golfer's bag during a competitive round?**
   A. 12
   B. 13
   C. 14
   D. 15

10. **What is the name of the trophy awarded to the winner of The Open Championship?**
    A. Claret Jug
    B. Ryder Cup
    C. Wanamaker Trophy
    D. FedEx Cup

11. **Who is the youngest golfer to win a major championship?**
    A. Jordan Spieth
    B. Rory McIlroy
    C. Tiger Woods
    D. Young Tom Morris

12. **What is the term for when a golfer completes a hole in one shot?**
    A. Birdie
    B. Bogey
    C. Hole-in-one
    D. Par
13. **Which women's golfer has won the most major championships?**
    A. Annika Sörenstam
    B. Lorena Ochoa
    C. Kathy Whitworth
    D. Patty Berg
14. **What is the term for the area of closely mowed grass surrounding the hole?**
    A. Fairway
    B. Rough
    C. Fringe
    D. Green
15. **Which U.S. golfer famously won the 1999 Ryder Cup with a dramatic comeback?**
    A. Tiger Woods
    B. Phil Mickelson
    C. Justin Leonard
    D. Davis Love III

Answers Part 1: Golf Trivia

1. B. Birdie
2. B. Jack Nicklaus
3. True
4. B. Double Eagle (Albatross)
5. A. The Masters
6. C. Scotland
7. B. Green
8. B. Branden Grace (62 in the 2017 Open Championship)
9. C. 14
10. A. Claret Jug
11. D. Young Tom Morris (17 years old)
12. C. Hole-in-one
13. D. Patty Berg (15 major championships)
14. D. Green
15. C. Justin Leonard

Chapter 13: Animals

Fun Facts About Animals

1. A group of flamingos is called a "flamboyance," while a group of crows is called a "murder."
2. The heart of a blue whale, the largest animal on Earth, weighs about as much as a small car.
3. Octopuses have three hearts and blue blood: two hearts pump blood to the gills, and the third pumps it to the rest of the body.
4. Koalas have fingerprints that are so similar to humans that they can confuse crime scene investigators.
5. Elephants are the only animals that can't jump due to their sheer size and structure.
6. Sharks existed on Earth before dinosaurs; they have been around for over 400 million years.
7. Honey never spoils; archaeologists have found pots of honey in ancient Egyptian tombs that are still edible.
8. The mimic octopus can imitate the appearance and movement of over 15 different species, including jellyfish and sea snakes.
9. Sloths move so slowly that algae can grow on their fur, helping them blend into the trees.
10. A newborn kangaroo, called a "joey," is the size of a jellybean when it is born.

Trivia Quiz Part 1: Animals

1. **What is the fastest land animal?**
   A. Cheetah
   B. Lion
   C. Gazelle
   D. Greyhound
2. **Which bird is known for its ability to mimic human speech?**
   A. Parrot
   B. Crow
   C. Mockingbird
   D. Raven
3. **True or False: Dolphins are mammals.**
4. **What is the largest species of shark?**
   A. Great White Shark
   B. Hammerhead Shark
   C. Whale Shark
   D. Tiger Shark
5. **What is the only continent where penguins live in the wild?**
   A. Asia
   B. Africa
   C. Antarctica
   D. South America
6. **What is the term for a baby kangaroo?**
   A. Cub
   B. Joey
   C. Kit
   D. Calf

7. **Which animal has the longest lifespan?**
   A. Bowhead Whale
   B. Giant Tortoise
   C. Greenland Shark
   D. Elephant
8. **How many legs does a spider have?**
   A. 6
   B. 8
   C. 10
   D. 12
9. **What is the largest land animal?**
   A. Elephant
   B. Hippopotamus
   C. Giraffe
   D. Rhinoceros
10. **Which bird is often associated with delivering babies in folklore?**
    A. Swan
    B. Crane
    C. Stork
    D. Dove
11. **What is the only mammal capable of true flight?**
    A. Squirrel
    B. Bat
    C. Flying Lemur
    D. Gliding Possum
12. **What colour is a polar bear's skin under its fur?**
    A. White
    B. Pink
    C. Black
    D. Grey

13. **Which animal is the largest reptile in the world?**
    A. Saltwater Crocodile
    B. Komodo Dragon
    C. Green Anaconda
    D. Leatherback Turtle
14. **What is a group of lions called?**
    A: Herd
    B. Pride
    C. Pack
    D. Flock
15. **What is the name of the tallest animal in the world?**
    A. Elephant
    B. Giraffe
    C. Ostrich
    D. Camel

Answers Part 1: Animals

1. A. Cheetah
2. A. Parrot
3. True
4. C. Whale Shark
5. C. Antarctica
6. B. Joey
7. C. Greenland Shark (over 400 years)
8. B. 8
9. A. Elephant
10. C. Stork
11. B. Bat
12. C. Black
13. A. Saltwater Crocodile
14. B. Pride
15. B. Giraffe

More Fun Facts About Animals

1. The fingerprints of a gorilla are so similar to humans that they can be mistaken at crime scenes.
2. Sea otters hold hands while sleeping to keep from drifting apart.
3. Male penguins propose to females by presenting them with a pebble, which the female uses to build a nest if she accepts.
4. Ostriches can run faster than horses, reaching speeds of up to 60 km/h (37 mph).

5. Hummingbirds are the only birds that can fly backward.
6. The loudest animal in the world is the sperm whale, which can produce sounds up to 230 decibels, louder than a jet engine.
7. A snail can sleep for up to three years if conditions are unfavourable for survival.
8. Crocodiles can go for months without eating due to their slow metabolism.
9. The brain of an octopus has more neurons than a human brain, making them highly intelligent and capable of problem-solving.
10. The Axolotl, a type of salamander, can regenerate its limbs, tail, heart, spinal cord, and even parts of its brain.

Trivia Quiz Part 2: Animals

1. **What is the largest species of bear?**
   A. Grizzly Bear
   B. Kodiak Bear
   C. Polar Bear
   D. Black Bear
2. **Which animal has the highest blood pressure?**
   A. Elephant
   B. Blue Whale
   C. Giraffe
   D. Shark

3. **True or False: Camels store water in their humps.**
4. **What is the fastest bird in the world?**
   A. Golden Eagle
   B. Peregrine Falcon
   C. Albatross
   D. Swift
5. **Which animal has the longest migration in the world?**
   A. Arctic Tern
   B. Humpback Whale
   C. Monarch Butterfly
   D. Leatherback Turtle
6. **What is the name of a baby fox?**
   A. Pup
   B. Kit
   C. Cub
   D. Joey
7. **Which sea creature is known for having no brain or heart?**
   A. Starfish
   B. Jellyfish
   C. Sea Cucumber
   D. Sponge
8. **What is the name of the smallest mammal in the world?**
   A. Bumblebee Bat
   B. Pygmy Shrew
   C. Sugar Glider
   D. Dwarf Hamster

9. **How many hearts does an octopus have?**
   A. 1
   B. 2
   C. 3
   D. 4
10. **Which animal is known to have the strongest bite force?**
    A. Crocodile
    B. Lion
    C. Great White Shark
    D. Hippopotamus
11. **What is the only known venomous mammal?**
    A. Platypus
    B. Mole
    C. Shrew
    D. Bat
12. **Which insect is known to have the longest lifespan?**
    A. Termite Queen
    B. Cicada
    C. Mayfly
    D. Dragonfly
13. **What is the name of the largest species of snake?**
    A. Reticulated Python
    B. Green Anaconda
    C. King Cobra
    D. Boa Constrictor
14. **What is a group of owls called?**
    A. Parliament
    B. Flock
    C. Colony
    D. Court

15. **Which animal holds the title for the fastest marine swimmer?**
    A. Sailfish
    B. Marlin
    C. Dolphin
    D. Tuna

Answers Part 2: Animals T

1. **C. Polar Bear**
2. **C. Giraffe** (to pump blood up their long necks)
3. **False** (Camels store fat, not water, in their humps.)
4. **B. Peregrine Falcon** (dives at speeds over 240 mph)
5. **A. Arctic Tern** (migrates up to 70,000 km annually)
6. **B. Kit**
7. **B. Jellyfish**
8. **A. Bumblebee Bat**
9. **C. 3**
10. **A. Crocodile**
11. **A. Platypus**
12. **A. Termite Queen** (up to 50 years)
13. **B. Green Anaconda**
14. **A. Parliament**
15. **A. Sailfish** (can swim up to 68 mph)

Even More Fun Facts About Animals

1. The mantis shrimp can punch with the force of a bullet, breaking shells and even aquarium glass.
2. Cows have best friends and become stressed when they are separated from them.
3. The wandering albatross has the largest wingspan of any bird, measuring up to 12 feet.
4. A group of hedgehogs is called a "prickle."
5. The heart of a shrimp is located in its head.

6. Some fish, like clownfish, can change their sex during their lifetime for reproductive purposes.
7. Pigeons can recognise themselves in mirrors, a sign of self-awareness that only a few animals possess.
8. The kakapo, a nocturnal parrot from New Zealand, is critically endangered, with fewer than 300 individuals remaining.
9. Vampire bats share blood meals with less fortunate colony members, showing a form of social cooperation.
10. Sea turtles have been around for over 100 million years, predating most species of dinosaurs.

Trivia Quiz Part 3: Animals

1. **What is the largest living reptile?**
   A. Green Anaconda
   B. Saltwater Crocodile
   C. Komodo Dragon
   D. Leatherback Turtle
2. **Which mammal is known for its laughter-like sounds when it communicates?**
   A. Dolphin
   B. Hyena
   C. Monkey
   D. Otter
3. **True or False: All bees die after they sting.**
4. **Which bird is the smallest in the world?**
   A. Hummingbird
   B. Finch
   C. Wren
   D. Sparrow
5. **Which animal has no stomach and digests its food in its intestines?**
   A. Seahorse
   B. Jellyfish
   C. Starfish
   D. Shrimp
6. **What is the name of the fastest land insect?**
   A. Tiger Beetle
   B. Cockroach
   C. Ant
   D. Grasshopper

7. **Which mammal can hold its breath the longest?**
    A. Sperm Whale
    B. Sea Otter
    C. Blue Whale
    D. Elephant Seal

8. **How many chambers does a cow's stomach have?**
    A. 2
    B. 3
    C. 4
    D. 5

9. **Which animal has the largest eyes in the animal kingdom?**
    A. Ostrich
    B. Giant Squid
    C. Elephant
    D. Blue Whale

10. **What is a group of jellyfish called?**
    A. Swarm
    B. Flock
    C. Bloom
    D. Colony

11. **What is the name of the only poisonous bird?**
    A. Cassowary
    B. Pitohui
    C. Harpy Eagle
    D. Kookaburra

12. **Which animal sleeps with one eye open?**
    A. Shark
    B. Dolphin
    C. Crocodile
    D. Seal

13. **Which is the heaviest flying bird?**
    A. Andean Condor
    B. Trumpeter Swan
    C. Kori Bustard
    D. Albatross
14. **What type of animal is a "bonobo"?**
    A. Monkey
    B. Ape
    C. Lemur
    D. Rodent
15. **What is the term for animals that are active during twilight?**
    A. Diurnal
    B. Nocturnal
    C. Crepuscular
    D. Arboreal

Answers Part 3: Animals

1. **B. Saltwater Crocodile**
2. **B. Hyena**
3. **False** (Only honeybees die after stinging, not all bees.)
4. **A. Hummingbird**
5. **A. Seahorse**
6. **A. Tiger Beetle** (can run at speeds of up to 5.6 mph)
7. **A. Sperm Whale** (can hold its breath for over 90 minutes)
8. **C. 4**
9. **B. Giant Squid** (eyes can be up to 10 inches across)
10. **C. Bloom**
11. **B. Pitohui** (found in New Guinea, its feathers contain toxins)
12. **B. Dolphin**
13. **C. Kori Bustard** (can weigh up to 44 pounds)
14. **B. Ape** (closely related to chimpanzees)
15. **C. Crepuscular**

Chapter 14: Space

Fun Facts About Space

1. Space is completely silent because there is no air to carry sound waves.
2. A day on Venus is longer than a year on Venus because it takes the planet longer to rotate on its axis than to complete an orbit around the Sun.
3. The Moon is slowly moving away from Earth at a rate of about 3.8 centimetres per year.
4. Jupiter has the most moons of any planet in the solar system, with over 90 confirmed moons.
5. A teaspoon of a neutron star would weigh about 6 billion tons on Earth due to its extreme density.
6. The Sun accounts for about 99.86% of the total mass of the solar system.
7. The largest volcano in the solar system is Olympus Mons on Mars, standing about three times the height of Mount Everest.
8. The Milky Way galaxy is on a collision course with the Andromeda galaxy, though the collision won't occur for about 4.5 billion years.
9. Saturn's rings are made of billions of particles of ice, rock, and dust, ranging in size from tiny grains to objects as large as mountains.
10. A single day on Uranus lasts 17 hours and 14 minutes, but a year on Uranus is 84 Earth years long.

Trivia Quiz Part 1: Space

1. **What is the largest planet in our solar system?**
   A. Earth
   B. Jupiter
   C. Saturn
   D. Neptune
2. **What is the name of the galaxy we live in?**
   A. Andromeda
   B. Milky Way
   C. Whirlpool
   D. Triangulum
3. **True or False: The Sun is a planet.**
4. **Which planet is known as the "Red Planet"?**
   A. Venus
   B. Mars
   C. Jupiter
   D. Mercury
5. **What is the term for a star that has exploded?**
   A. Black hole
   B. Supernova
   C. Nebula
   D. Quasar
6. **Which planet has the shortest day in the solar system?**
   A. Venus
   B. Jupiter
   C. Saturn
   D. Neptune

7. **What is the name of the first artificial satellite to orbit Earth?**
   A. Apollo 11
   B. Sputnik 1
   C. Voyager 1
   D. Luna 2

8. **What is the coldest planet in our solar system?**
   A. Uranus
   B. Neptune
   C. Pluto
   D. Saturn

9. **How long does it take for light from the Sun to reach Earth?**
   A. 8 seconds
   B. 8 minutes
   C. 8 hours
   D. 8 days

10. **What is the term for a rocky body that orbits the Sun and is smaller than a planet?**
    A. Meteor
    B. Comet
    C. Asteroid
    D. Satellite

11. **Which planet has the tallest mountain in the solar system?**
    A. Earth
    B. Mars
    C. Venus
    D. Mercury

12. **What is the name of the largest moon of Saturn?**
    A. Titan
    B. Europa
    C. Callisto
    D. Ganymede
13. **What is a black hole?**
    A. A type of star
    B. A collapsed star with intense gravity
    C. A hole in space
    D. A large asteroid
14. **Which spacecraft was the first to land on the Moon?**
    A. Apollo 11
    B. Sputnik 2
    C. Voyager 1
    D. Luna 9
15. **What is the approximate age of the universe?**
    A. 4.5 billion years
    B. 13.8 billion years
    C. 1 trillion years
    D. 100 million years

Answers Part 1: Space

1. B. Jupiter
2. B. Milky Way
3. False
4. B. Mars
5. B. Supernova
6. B. Jupiter (A day is about 10 hours.)
7. B. Sputnik 1
8. A. Uranus
9. B. 8 minutes
10. C. Asteroid
11. B. Mars (Olympus Mons)
12. A. Titan
13. B. A collapsed star with intense gravity
14. A. Apollo 11
15. B. 13.8 billion years

Even More Fun Facts About Space

1. A year on Mercury is only 88 Earth days long, but a single day on Mercury (sunrise to sunrise) lasts 176 Earth days.
2. The Moon is the fifth-largest natural satellite in the solar system and has no atmosphere, which is why its footprints will last for millions of years.
3. The Great Red Spot on Jupiter is a storm larger than Earth that has been raging for at least 350 years.
4. The International Space Station (ISS) travels at a speed of about 28,000 km/h (17,500 mph), orbiting Earth roughly every 90 minutes.

5. There are more stars in the universe than grains of sand on all the beaches of Earth.
6. The first human-made object to reach space was the German V-2 rocket in 1944.
7. Mars has the largest dust storms in the solar system, sometimes covering the entire planet and lasting for months.
8. The Kuiper Belt is a region of the solar system beyond Neptune that contains icy bodies, including Pluto.
9. Voyager 1, launched in 1977, is the most distant human-made object from Earth and has entered interstellar space.
10. A pulsar is a type of neutron star that emits beams of radiation, appearing to pulse as it rotates.

Trivia Quiz Part 2: Space

1. **What is the smallest planet in our solar system?**
   A. Mercury
   B. Mars
   C. Pluto
   D. Venus
2. **What is the name of the boundary where a black hole's gravity is so strong that nothing can escape?**
   A. Event Horizon
   B. Schwarzschild Radius
   C. Singularity
   D. Gravitational Limit
3. **True or False: Neptune is the windiest planet in the solar system.**
4. **What is the name of the largest moon in the solar system?**
   A. Titan
   B. Ganymede
   C. Callisto
   D. Europa
5. **What is the main component of the Sun?**
   A. Helium
   B. Hydrogen
   C. Carbon
   D. Oxygen
6. **Which planet spins on its side, with its axis nearly horizontal to its orbit?**
   A. Venus
   B. Uranus
   C. Saturn
   D. Neptune

7. **What is the name of the spacecraft that carried the first humans to land on the Moon?**
   A. Apollo 10
   B. Apollo 11
   C. Apollo 13
   D. Apollo 14

8. **What is the brightest star in the night sky?**
   A. Betelgeuse
   B. Sirius
   C. Polaris
   D. Vega

9. **What is the term for the explosion of a massive star?**
   A. Black Hole
   B. Supernova
   C. White Dwarf
   D. Nebula

10. **Which planet is known for having a hexagonal storm at its north pole?**
    A. Jupiter
    B. Saturn
    C. Neptune
    D. Uranus

11. **What is the closest galaxy to the Milky Way?**
    A. Sombrero Galaxy
    B. Andromeda Galaxy
    C. Whirlpool Galaxy
    D. Triangulum Galaxy

12. **What is the name of the first living creature sent into space?**
    A. Laika
    B. Ham
    C. Albert I
    D. Felicette

13. How many Earths could fit inside the Sun?
    A. 1,000
    B. 10,000
    C. 1 million
    D. 100 million
14. What is the name of the largest asteroid in the asteroid belt?
    A. Vesta
    B. Ceres
    C. Pallas
    D. Hygiea
15. Which planet has the most volcanoes?
    A. Earth
    B. Venus
    C. Mars
    D. Io

Answers Part 2: Space

1. **A. Mercury**
2. **A. Event Horizon**
3. **True** (Neptune has winds reaching 2,100 km/h or 1,300 mph.)
4. **B. Ganymede**
5. **B. Hydrogen**
6. **B. Uranus**
7. **B. Apollo 11**
8. **B. Sirius**
9. **B. Supernova**
10. **B. Saturn**
11. **B. Andromeda Galaxy**
12. **A. Laika** (a Soviet dog sent aboard Sputnik 2 in 1957)
13. **C. 1 million**
14. **B. Ceres**
15. **B. Venus** (over 1,600 volcanoes)

Chapter 15: News and Pop Culture

Fun Facts About News and Pop Culture

1. The first televised news broadcast was aired on July 1, 1941, in the United States by NBC.
2. The Beatles hold the record for the most number-one hits on the Billboard Hot 100 chart, with 20 songs reaching the top spot.
3. The Academy Awards, also known as the Oscars, were first held in 1929 and lasted only 15 minutes.
4. The world's first selfie is believed to have been taken in 1839 by Robert Cornelius, using early photography technology.
5. The most-watched television broadcast in history was the 1969 Moon landing, with over 600 million viewers worldwide.
6. The first YouTube video, titled *Me at the Zoo*, was uploaded on April 23, 2005, by one of the platform's co-founders, Jawed Karim.
7. The highest-grossing movie of all time (adjusted for inflation) is *Gone with the Wind* (1939).
8. The most-followed person on Instagram as of 2024 is Cristiano Ronaldo, with over 600 million followers.
9. The phrase "breaking news" originated in the 19th century when newspapers would interrupt regular print schedules to report urgent stories.
10. The longest-running scripted TV show in history is *The Simpsons*, which debuted in 1989 and continues to air today.

Trivia Quiz Part 1: News and Pop Culture

1. **Who was the first actor to win an Academy Award for Best Actor?**
   A. Clark Gable
   B. Emil Jannings
   C. Charlie Chaplin
   D. Douglas Fairbanks
2. **What year did the Berlin Wall fall, marking the end of the Cold War?**
   A. 1987
   B. 1988
   C. 1989
   D. 1990
3. **True or False: Facebook was originally called "The Facebook."**
4. **Which music artist has won the most Grammy Awards in history?**
   A. Beyoncé
   B. Quincy Jones
   C. Georg Solti
   D. Taylor Swift
5. **What was the first video game ever created?**
   A. Pong
   B. Space Invaders
   C. Tennis for Two
   D. Pac-Man
6. **Who was the first person to reach 1 million followers on Twitter?**
   A. Ashton Kutcher
   B. Lady Gaga
   C. Barack Obama
   D. Justin Bieber

7. **What year did Netflix begin streaming content?**
   A. 2005
   B. 2007
   C. 2009
   D. 2010
8. **What is the best-selling book series of all time?**
   A. Harry Potter
   B. The Lord of the Rings
   C. The Chronicles of Narnia
   D. Twilight
9. **Who was the first woman to host a late-night talk show on network television?**
   A. Joan Rivers
   B. Ellen DeGeneres
   C. Chelsea Handler
   D. Samantha Bee
10. **Which social media platform introduced hashtags?**
   A. Facebook
   B. Instagram
   C. Twitter
   D. Snapchat
11. **What year was Google founded?**
   A. 1996
   B. 1998
   C. 2000
   D. 2001

12. **Who is the highest-paid actor in history (as of 2024)?**
    A. Dwayne "The Rock" Johnson
    B. Robert Downey Jr.
    C. Tom Cruise
    D. Leonardo DiCaprio
13. **Which TV series finale is the most-watched in history?**
    A. *Friends*
    B. *MASH**
    C. *Game of Thrones*
    D. *Breaking Bad*
14. **What is the name of the longest-running comic strip in history?**
    A. *Garfield*
    B. *Peanuts*
    C. *The Family Circus*
    D. *The Katzenjammer Kids*
15. **Which singer holds the record for the fastest-selling album of all time?**
    A. Adele
    B. Taylor Swift
    C. Michael Jackson
    D. NSYNC

Answers Part 1: News and Pop Culture

1. B. Emil Jannings
2. C. 1989
3. True
4. C. Georg Solti (31 Grammys)
5. C. Tennis for Two (created in 1958)
6. A. Ashton Kutcher
7. B. 2007
8. A. Harry Potter
9. A. Joan Rivers
10. C. Twitter
11. B. 1998
12. A. Dwayne "The Rock" Johnson
13. B. *MASH**
14. D. *The Katzenjammer Kids*
15. C. Michael Jackson (*Thriller*)

Even More Fun Facts About News and Pop Culture

1. The first daily newspaper, *The Daily Courant*, was published in London in 1702.
2. *The Wizard of Oz* (1939) was the first movie to be broadcast on television.
3. The original Twitter logo was named "Larry the Bird," inspired by basketball legend Larry Bird.
4. Elvis Presley made his television debut in 1956 on *The Ed Sullivan Show*, propelling him to national fame.
5. The most-streamed song of all time (as of 2024) is "Blinding Lights" by The Weeknd.

6. Walt Disney was awarded more Academy Awards than anyone else in history, with a total of 26 Oscars.
7. The first colour TV broadcast occurred in 1951, showing the CBS program *Premiere*.
8. The most-watched sporting event in history is the 2008 Beijing Olympics opening ceremony, with over 2 billion viewers.
9. The first-ever email was sent in 1971 by Ray Tomlinson to himself.
10. *Friends* was almost titled *Insomnia Café* during its early production stages.

Trivia Quiz Part 2: News and Pop Culture

1. **Who directed the movie *Titanic*?**
   A. Steven Spielberg
   B. James Cameron
   C. Ridley Scott
   D. Martin Scorsese
2. **What was the first song ever played on MTV?**
   A. "Like a Virgin" by Madonna
   B. "Video Killed the Radio Star" by The Buggles
   C. "Thriller" by Michael Jackson
   D. "Take On Me" by A-ha
3. **True or False: Apple's original logo featured an image of Isaac Newton.**
4. **Who became the first woman to win an Oscar for Best Director?**
   A. Sofia Coppola
   B. Kathryn Bigelow
   C. Jane Campion
   D. Greta Gerwig
5. **What year did the first Harry Potter book release?**
   A. 1995
   B. 1997
   C. 1999
   D. 2000
6. **Which artist painted the ceiling of the Sistine Chapel?**
   A. Leonardo da Vinci
   B. Raphael
   C. Michelangelo
   D. Donatello

7. **What is the longest-running soap opera in history?**
   A. *Coronation Street*
   B. *Guiding Light*
   C. *General Hospital*
   D. *Days of Our Lives*
8. **What is the highest-grossing animated film of all time (as of 2024)?**
   A. *Frozen*
   B. *The Lion King* (2019)
   C. *Frozen II*
   D. *Toy Story 4*
9. **Who was the first performer to headline the Super Bowl halftime show?**
   A. Michael Jackson
   B. Diana Ross
   C. Prince
   D. Gloria Estefan
10. **What was the first film to gross over $1 billion worldwide?**
    A. *Jurassic Park*
    B. *Avatar*
    C. *Titanic*
    D. *The Godfather*
11. **Which author holds the record for the most books sold in history?**
    A. J.K. Rowling
    B. Agatha Christie
    C. Stephen King
    D. William Shakespeare

12. **What is the longest-running scripted primetime TV series in the U.S.?**
    A. *Law & Order*
    B. *The Simpsons*
    C. *Grey's Anatomy*
    D. *NCIS*
13. **What is the most-watched YouTube video of all time?**
    A. "Gangnam Style" by Psy
    B. "Baby Shark Dance"
    C. "Despacito" by Luis Fonsi
    D. "See You Again" by Wiz Khalifa
14. **Which Netflix series was the first to win an Emmy for Outstanding Drama Series?**
    A. *Stranger Things*
    B. *The Crown*
    C. *House of Cards*
    D. *Orange Is the New Black*
15. **What is the name of the highest-selling album of all time?**
    A. *The Wall* by Pink Floyd
    B. *Back in Black* by AC/DC
    C. *Thriller* by Michael Jackson
    D. *Rumours* by Fleetwood Mac

Answers Part 2: News and Pop Culture

1. B. James Cameron
2. B. "Video Killed the Radio Star" by The Buggles
3. True
4. B. Kathryn Bigelow (for *The Hurt Locker* in 2010)
5. B. 1997
6. C. Michelangelo
7. B. *Guiding Light*
8. C. *Frozen II*
9. A. Michael Jackson
10. C. *Titanic*
11. B. Agatha Christie
12. B. *The Simpsons*
13. B. "Baby Shark Dance"
14. C. *House of Cards*
15. C. *Thriller* by Michael Jackson

Even More Fun Facts About News and Pop Culture

1. The most expensive movie ever made is *Pirates of the Caribbean: On Stranger Tides* (2011), with a budget of $379 million.
2. Beyoncé's *Renaissance World Tour* (2023) is the highest-grossing tour by a solo artist in history.
3. The first television commercial aired on July 1, 1941, for Bulova Watches and cost $9.
4. Oprah Winfrey was the first African American woman to own her own production company, Harpo Productions, founded in 1986.
5. The world's most visited museum is the Louvre in Paris, home to the *Mona Lisa*.
6. Twitter's character limit was originally 140 but increased to 280 in 2017.
7. *Avatar* (2009) was the first movie to cross $2 billion at the global box office.
8. The first video uploaded to TikTok was in 2016, and the platform has since become one of the fastest-growing social media apps.
9. Walt Disney World in Florida is roughly the same size as San Francisco, covering about 40 square miles.
10. The longest-running Broadway show is *The Phantom of the Opera*, which debuted in 1988 and closed in 2023.

Trivia Quiz Part 3: News and Pop Culture

1. **Which artist was the youngest to win the Grammy for Album of the Year?**
    A. Taylor Swift
    B. Billie Eilish
    C. Olivia Rodrigo
    D. Lorde
2. **What is the longest-running film franchise in history?**
    A. *Star Wars*
    B. *James Bond*
    C. *Marvel Cinematic Universe*
    D. *Harry Potter*
3. **True or False:** *Friends* **was the first TV show to feature a same-sex wedding.**
4. **Who was the first woman to appear on the cover of** *Rolling Stone* **magazine?**
    A. Tina Turner
    B. Janis Joplin
    C. Aretha Franklin
    D. Joni Mitchell
5. **Which movie won the first-ever Academy Award for Best Picture?**
    A. *Wings*
    B. *Sunrise*
    C. *Metropolis*
    D. *The Broadway Melody*
6. **Which artist had the first music video to reach 1 billion views on YouTube?**
    A. Psy
    B. Justin Bieber
    C. Katy Perry
    D. Lady Gaga

7. **What year did the first iPhone release?**
   A. 2005
   B. 2007
   C. 2009
   D. 2010
8. **Who was the first African American to win an Oscar for Best Actor?**
   A. Denzel Washington
   B. Sidney Poitier
   C. Morgan Freeman
   D. Jamie Foxx
9. **What is the most-watched TV series on Netflix (as of 2024)?**
   A. *Stranger Things*
   B. *Squid Game*
   C. *Wednesday*
   D. *Bridgerton*
10. **What is the highest-selling video game of all time?**
    A. *Minecraft*
    B. *Grand Theft Auto V*
    C. *Tetris*
    D. *Mario Kart 8 Deluxe*
11. **What was the first streaming series to win an Emmy for Outstanding Comedy Series?**
    A. *The Marvelous Mrs. Maisel*
    B. *Ted Lasso*
    C. *Schitt's Creek*
    D. *Orange Is the New Black*

12. **Who was the first woman inducted into the Rock and Roll Hall of Fame?**
    A. Aretha Franklin
    B. Janis Joplin
    C. Tina Turner
    D. Carole King
13. **Which actor has the most Oscar nominations of all time?**
    A. Leonardo DiCaprio
    B. Meryl Streep
    C. Jack Nicholson
    D. Katharine Hepburn
14. **Which social media platform reached 1 billion users the fastest?**
    A. Instagram
    B. TikTok
    C. Facebook
    D. YouTube
15. **What is the most expensive painting ever sold at auction?**
    A. *The Scream* by Edvard Munch
    B. *Mona Lisa* by Leonardo da Vinci
    C. *Salvator Mundi* by Leonardo da Vinci
    D. *Starry Night* by Vincent van Gogh

Answers Part 3: News and Pop Culture

1. **B. Billie Eilish** (for *When We All Fall Asleep, Where Do We Go?* at age 18)
2. **B. *James Bond*** (first film released in 1962)
3. **True** (*Friends* featured Carol and Susan's wedding in 1996.)
4. **B. Janis Joplin**
5. **A. *Wings*** (1927)
6. **A. Psy** ("Gangnam Style")
7. **B. 2007**
8. **B. Sidney Poitier** (*Lilies of the Field*, 1964)
9. **B. *Squid Game***
10. **A. *Minecraft***
11. **A. *The Marvelous Mrs. Maisel***
12. **A. Aretha Franklin** (1987)
13. **B. Meryl Streep** (21 nominations)
14. **B. TikTok**
15. **C. *Salvator Mundi* by Leonardo da Vinci** ($450.3 million in 2017)

Chapter 16: Expanded History

Fun Facts About Expanded History

1. Cleopatra lived closer in time to the Moon landing (1969) than to the construction of the Great Pyramid of Giza (2560 BCE).
2. Napoleon Bonaparte was once attacked by a horde of rabbits during a hunting expedition.
3. The shortest war in history was between Britain and Zanzibar on August 27, 1896, lasting only 38 minutes.
4. Albert Einstein was offered the presidency of Israel in 1952 but declined the role.
5. The Eiffel Tower was initially intended to be dismantled after 20 years, but it was saved because it was repurposed as a radio tower.
6. The Great Fire of London in 1666 destroyed 80% of the city but resulted in only six recorded deaths.
7. The Hundred Years' War between England and France actually lasted 116 years, from 1337 to 1453.
8. The first known city in history is Uruk, located in modern-day Iraq, which dates back to around 4000 BCE.
9. During World War II, the British government asked citizens to donate metal items, including pots and pans, to build airplanes.
10. The oldest written story in the world is the *Epic of Gilgamesh*, which dates back to around 2100 BCE.

Trivia Quiz Part 1: Expanded History

1. **Who was the first President of the United States?**
   A. George Washington
   B. Thomas Jefferson
   C. Abraham Lincoln
   D. John Adams
2. **What year did World War I begin?**
   A. 1912
   B. 1914
   C. 1916
   D. 1918
3. **True or False: The Great Wall of China can be seen from space.**
4. **Which famous explorer is credited with discovering America in 1492?**
   A. Vasco da Gama
   B. Christopher Columbus
   C. Ferdinand Magellan
   D. Marco Polo
5. **What was the name of the ship that transported the Pilgrims to America in 1620?**
   A. Santa Maria
   B. Mayflower
   C. Titanic
   D. Discovery
6. **Which ancient empire was ruled by Julius Caesar?**
   A. Greek Empire
   B. Roman Empire
   C. Persian Empire
   D. Ottoman Empire

7. **What year did the Berlin Wall fall?**
   A. 1987
   B. 1988
   C. 1989
   D. 1990
8. **Who was the first female Prime Minister of the United Kingdom?**
   A. Margaret Thatcher
   B. Queen Victoria
   C. Theresa May
   D. Elizabeth I
9. **What was the name of the ship Charles Darwin sailed on during his journey to the Galápagos Islands?**
   A. HMS Endeavour
   B. HMS Beagle
   C. HMS Victory
   D. HMS Challenger
10. **What was the first country to grant women the right to vote?**
    A. United States
    B. New Zealand
    C. Canada
    D. United Kingdom
11. **Who was assassinated in Sarajevo in 1914, sparking World War I?**
    A. Franz Ferdinand
    B. Otto von Bismarck
    C. Gavrilo Princip
    D. Nicholas II

12. **What was the primary material used to build the Great Wall of China?**
    A. Stone
    B. Brick
    C. Wood
    D. Earth
13. **What was the name of the Aztec capital city?**
    A. Machu Picchu
    B. Tenochtitlán
    C. Chichen Itza
    D. Cusco
14. **Which country gifted the Statue of Liberty to the United States?**
    A. United Kingdom
    B. France
    C. Italy
    D. Spain
15. **What was the name of the treaty that ended World War I?**
    A. Treaty of Versailles
    B. Treaty of Paris
    C. Treaty of Tordesillas
    D. Treaty of Ghent

Answers Part 1: Expanded History

1. **A. George Washington**
2. **B. 1914**
3. **False** (It cannot be seen with the naked eye from space.)
4. **B. Christopher Columbus**
5. **B. Mayflower**
6. **B. Roman Empire**
7. **C. 1989**
8. **A. Margaret Thatcher**
9. **B. HMS Beagle**
10. **B. New Zealand**
11. **A. Franz Ferdinand**
12. **D. Earth** (packed earth, later reinforced with stone and brick in some areas)
13. **B. Tenochtitlán**
14. **B. France**
15. **A. Treaty of Versailles**

Even More Fun Facts About Expanded History

1. Abraham Lincoln is enshrined in the National Wrestling Hall of Fame, having won nearly 300 matches in his wrestling career.
2. The famous explorer Marco Polo introduced pasta to Italy from China, although this claim remains debated by historians.
3. Iceland was the last European country to adopt surnames, and even today, most Icelanders use patronymic or matronymic naming conventions.

4. Leonardo da Vinci was ambidextrous and could write with one hand while drawing with the other simultaneously.
5. The Roman Colosseum was originally called the Flavian Amphitheatre and could hold up to 80,000 spectators.
6. During the Victorian era, people used to take photos with their deceased loved ones, a practice called post-mortem photography.
7. The first known Olympic Games were held in 776 BCE in Olympia, Greece, and featured only one event: a 192-meter footrace.
8. In medieval Europe, black pepper was so valuable it was used as currency.
9. Marie Curie is the only person to win Nobel Prizes in two different sciences (Physics and Chemistry).
10. Genghis Khan's empire was so vast that it covered 12 million square miles, making it the largest contiguous empire in history.

Trivia Quiz Part 2: Expanded History

1. **Who was the first emperor of Rome?**
   A. Julius Caesar
   B. Augustus
   C. Nero
   D. Caligula
2. **What year did the Titanic sink?**
   A. 1909
   B. 1911
   C. 1912
   D. 1915
3. **True or False: The Declaration of Independence was signed on July 4, 1776.**
4. **Which empire built the Machu Picchu?**
   A. Aztec
   B. Mayan
   C. Inca
   D. Olmec
5. **What city was famously destroyed by a volcanic eruption in 79 CE?**
   A. Athens
   B. Pompeii
   C. Rome
   D. Alexandria
6. **Who was the first person to circumnavigate the globe?**
   A. Christopher Columbus
   B. Ferdinand Magellan
   C. Vasco da Gama
   D. Juan Sebastián Elcano

7. **What year did the French Revolution begin?**
   A. 1787
   B. 1789
   C. 1793
   D. 1795
8. **What was the longest reigning dynasty in Chinese history?**
   A. Tang
   B. Ming
   C. Qing
   D. Zhou
9. **Which U.S. president is known for the Gettysburg Address?**
   A. George Washington
   B. Abraham Lincoln
   C. Thomas Jefferson
   D. Theodore Roosevelt
10. **What was the name of the plane that dropped the first atomic bomb?**
    A. Memphis Belle
    B. Spirit of St. Louis
    C. Enola Gay
    D. Bockscar
11. **Which ancient city was known as Byzantium before being renamed?**
    A. Rome
    B. Constantinople
    C. Athens
    D. Carthage
12. **What year did the Soviet Union collapse?**
    A. 1988
    B. 1989
    C. 1990
    D. 1991

13. **Who was the British Prime Minister during World War II?**
    A. Neville Chamberlain
    B. Winston Churchill
    C. Clement Attlee
    D. Margaret Thatcher
14. **What was the name of the ship Charles Lindbergh flew solo across the Atlantic?**
    A. Spirit of St. Louis
    B. Memphis Belle
    C. The Wright Flyer
    D. Skylark
15. **Which pharaoh was buried in the Great Pyramid of Giza?**
    A. Ramses II
    B. Tutankhamun
    C. Khufu
    D. Akhenaten

Answers Part 2: Expanded History

1. B. Augustus
2. C. 1912
3. False (It was adopted on July 4 but signed later.)
4. C. Inca
5. B. Pompeii
6. D. Juan Sebastián Elcano (Magellan died during the voyage.)
7. B. 1789
8. D. Zhou
9. B. Abraham Lincoln
10. C. Enola Gay
11. B. Constantinople
12. D. 1991
13. B. Winston Churchill
14. A. Spirit of St. Louis
15. C. Khufu

Even More Fun Facts About Expanded History

1. In 1518, a "dancing plague" occurred in Strasbourg, where dozens of people danced uncontrollably for days, and some even died from exhaustion.
2. The oldest known shoes, made from plant fibres, date back over 10,000 years and were discovered in a cave in Oregon.
3. The Library of Alexandria in ancient Egypt was one of the largest and most significant libraries of the ancient world, but its destruction remains shrouded in mystery.
4. During World War II, British intelligence used Monopoly games to smuggle maps, compasses, and money to help prisoners of war escape.
5. The Colosseum in Rome had a retractable roof system, operated by sailors, to protect spectators from the sun.
6. Vikings never wore horned helmets; this myth was popularised by 19th-century opera costumes.
7. The Great Fire of Chicago in 1871 was rumoured to have been started by a cow kicking over a lantern, though this story has been debunked.
8. Ancient Romans used urine as a cleaning product because it contains ammonia, a natural bleaching agent.
9. The guillotine was used in France as a method of execution until 1977.
10. Albert Einstein's brain was removed and preserved after his death for scientific study.

Trivia Quiz Part 3: Expanded History

1. **What year did World War II begin?**
    A. 1937
    B. 1938
    C. 1939
    D. 1940
2. **Which famous ruler was known as "The Sun King"?**
    A. Louis XIV
    B. Napoleon Bonaparte
    C. Henry VIII
    D. Charlemagne
3. **True or False: The Great Pyramid of Giza is the only surviving wonder of the ancient world.**
4. **What city was the capital of the Byzantine Empire?**
    A. Constantinople
    B. Rome
    C. Athens
    D. Carthage
5. **Which explorer was the first to reach the South Pole?**
    A. Robert Falcon Scott
    B. Roald Amundsen
    C. Ernest Shackleton
    D. James Cook
6. **Who was the longest-reigning monarch in British history (as of 2024)?**
    A. Queen Victoria
    B. King Charles III
    C. Queen Elizabeth II
    D. King George III

7. **What was the main cause of the War of the Roses?**
   A. Trade disputes
   B. Religious conflict
   C. Succession to the English throne
   D. Border disputes

8. **What year did the American Civil War begin?**
   A. 1859
   B. 1861
   C. 1863
   D. 1865

9. **Who painted the ceiling of the Sistine Chapel?**
   A. Leonardo da Vinci
   B. Michelangelo
   C. Raphael
   D. Donatello

10. **What was the capital of the Aztec Empire?**
    A. Cusco
    B. Tenochtitlán
    C. Chichen Itza
    D. Lima

11. **What major historical event is associated with October 29, 1929?**
    A. The end of World War I
    B. The Wall Street Crash
    C. The signing of the Treaty of Versailles
    D. The beginning of Prohibition

12. **Who was the last emperor of Russia?**
    A. Peter the Great
    B. Nicholas II
    C. Ivan the Terrible
    D. Alexander III

13. **Which empire built the Terracotta Army?**
    A. Roman Empire
    B. Egyptian Empire
    C. Qin Dynasty
    D. Han Dynasty
14. **What year did Nelson Mandela become President of South Africa?**
    A. 1990
    B. 1992
    C. 1994
    D. 1996
15. **What was the name of the first satellite launched into space?**
    A. Sputnik 1
    B. Apollo 11
    C. Vostok 1
    D. Explorer 1

Answers Part 3: Expanded History

1. C. 1939
2. A. Louis XIV
3. True
4. A. Constantinople
5. B. Roald Amundsen
6. C. Queen Elizabeth II (70 years and 214 days)
7. C. Succession to the English throne
8. B. 1861
9. B. Michelangelo
10. B. Tenochtitlán
11. B. The Wall Street Crash
12. B. Nicholas II
13. C. Qin Dynasty
14. C. 1994
15. A. Sputnik 1

Chapter 17: World Wars

Fun Facts About World Wars

1. The assassination of Archduke Franz Ferdinand of Austria-Hungary in 1914 sparked World War I, which lasted until 1918.
2. During World War II, Coca-Cola created Fanta to continue operations in Nazi Germany due to trade restrictions.
3. The Christmas Truce of 1914 during World War I saw soldiers from opposing sides emerge from their trenches to exchange gifts, sing carols, and play soccer.
4. The Allied invasion of Normandy on June 6, 1944, known as D-Day, was the largest amphibious invasion in history.
5. The term "Blitzkrieg," meaning "lightning war," was a German military tactic emphasising speed and surprise.
6. The Treaty of Versailles officially ended World War I but is often cited as a cause of World War II due to its harsh reparations on Germany.
7. Anne Frank's diary, written while hiding from the Nazis during World War II, has become one of the most famous firsthand accounts of the Holocaust.
8. The first tanks used in warfare were deployed by the British during the Battle of the Somme in 1916.
9. The atomic bombs dropped on Hiroshima and Nagasaki in 1945 led to Japan's surrender, effectively ending World War II.

10. The League of Nations was formed after World War I to prevent future wars but was replaced by the United Nations after World War II.

Trivia Quiz Part 1: World Wars

1. **Which country was Archduke Franz Ferdinand from?**
   A. Germany
   B. Austria-Hungary
   C. Serbia
   D. Russia
2. **What year did World War I end?**
   A. 1916
   B. 1917
   C. 1918
   D. 1919
3. **True or False: The sinking of the Titanic led to the U.S. joining World War I.**
4. **What was the name of the British Prime Minister during World War II?**
   A. Neville Chamberlain
   B. Winston Churchill
   C. Clement Attlee
   D. Stanley Baldwin
5. **Which countries made up the Axis Powers in World War II?**
   A. Germany, Italy, Japan
   B. Germany, Russia, Japan
   C. Italy, France, Germany
   D. Germany, Austria-Hungary, Italy

6. **What event prompted the United States to enter World War II?**
    A. The bombing of London
    B. The assassination of Franz Ferdinand
    C. The attack on Pearl Harbor
    D. The invasion of Poland
7. **What was the code name for the Allied invasion of Normandy?**
    A. Operation Torch
    B. Operation Overlord
    C. Operation Market Garden
    D. Operation Neptune
8. **What was the largest battle of World War I?**
    A. Battle of Verdun
    B. Battle of the Somme
    C. Battle of Gallipoli
    D. Battle of Ypres
9. **Who was the leader of Nazi Germany during World War II?**
    A. Joseph Stalin
    B. Adolf Hitler
    C. Benito Mussolini
    D. Hirohito
10. **Which treaty ended World War I?**
    A. Treaty of Paris
    B. Treaty of Versailles
    C. Treaty of Ghent
    D. Treaty of Tordesillas
11. **What year was the United Nations established?**
    A. 1944
    B. 1945
    C. 1946
    D. 1947

12. **What was the primary goal of the Manhattan Project?**
    A. Developing nuclear weapons
    B. Building tanks
    C. Creating radar technology
    D. Advancing aircraft design
13. **Which country suffered the highest military casualties in World War II?**
    A. Germany
    B. United States
    C. Soviet Union
    D. Japan
14. **What was the name of the German air force during World War II?**
    A. Wehrmacht
    B. Luftwaffe
    C. Panzer Corps
    D. Gestapo
15. **What was the "Zimmermann Telegram"?**
    A. A peace proposal from Germany
    B. A German message encouraging Mexico to join the war against the U.S.
    C. A secret message from Russia to Germany
    D. A British communication to the Allies

Answers Part 1: World Wars

1. B. Austria-Hungary
2. C. 1918
3. False (It was the sinking of the Lusitania that influenced U.S. involvement in World War I.)
4. B. Winston Churchill
5. A. Germany, Italy, Japan
6. C. The attack on Pearl Harbor
7. B. Operation Overlord
8. B. Battle of the Somme
9. B. Adolf Hitler
10. B. Treaty of Versailles
11. B. 1945
12. A. Developing nuclear weapons
13. C. Soviet Union (estimated 8.6 million military deaths)
14. B. Luftwaffe
15. B. A German message encouraging Mexico to join the war against the U.S.

Even More Fun Facts About World Wars

1. The "No Man's Land" in World War I was often only a few hundred yards wide but was filled with barbed wire, shell craters, and trenches.
2. The Treaty of Versailles included a "war guilt clause" that blamed Germany for World War I, fuelling resentment and economic hardship in the country.
3. The Enigma machine, used by Nazi Germany to encode messages during World War II, was famously decrypted by Alan Turing and his team at Bletchley Park.
4. During World War II, the Japanese "Balloon Bombs" were designed to drift across the Pacific and cause damage in the United States.
5. World War I saw the first use of chemical weapons, including chlorine and mustard gas. Gas masks became an essential part of a soldier's gear.
6. In World War II, Operation Barbarossa, the German invasion of the Soviet Union, was the largest military operation in history in terms of manpower and casualties.
7. Women played crucial roles in both World Wars, serving as nurses, factory workers, codebreakers, and even pilots in some countries.
8. During World War II, rationing was implemented in many countries, with citizens limited in their use of meat, sugar, and gasoline.
9. The first-ever use of tanks in warfare occurred during the Battle of Flers-Courcelette in 1916 during World War I.

10. The Battle of Stalingrad (1942-1943) was one of the deadliest battles in history, with nearly 2 million casualties.

Trivia Quiz Part 2: World Wars

1. **What year did the U.S. enter World War I?**
   A. 1915
   B. 1916
   C. 1917
   D. 1918
2. **What was the name of the German plan to invade France through Belgium in World War I?**
   A. Moltke Plan
   B. Schlieffen Plan
   C. Ludendorff Plan
   D. Hindenburg Plan
3. **True or False: Adolf Hitler served as a soldier in World War I.**
4. **What was the primary purpose of the Maginot Line?**
   A. To prevent invasions by sea
   B. To defend France from Germany
   C. To separate Austria and Hungary
   D. To secure Italy's northern border

5. **Which battle marked the turning point of World War II in the Pacific?**
   A. Battle of Midway
   B. Battle of Iwo Jima
   C. Battle of Okinawa
   D. Battle of Guadalcanal

6. **Which Allied leader was known as the "Desert Fox"?**
   A. Bernard Montgomery
   B. Erwin Rommel
   C. Dwight D. Eisenhower
   D. George S. Patton

7. **What year was the atomic bomb dropped on Hiroshima?**
   A. 1943
   B. 1944
   C. 1945
   D. 1946

8. **What was the name of the military operation to evacuate Allied soldiers from Dunkirk in 1940?**
   A. Operation Torch
   B. Operation Dynamo
   C. Operation Sea Lion
   D. Operation Husky

9. **Who was the U.S. president during most of World War II?**
   A. Woodrow Wilson
   B. Franklin D. Roosevelt
   C. Harry S. Truman
   D. Herbert Hoover

10. **What was the nickname given to the German submarines used during World War I and II?**
    A. U-boats
    B. Kriegsmarine
    C. Wolf Pack
    D. Schnellboot

11. **What year did the Treaty of Versailles come into effect?**
    A. 1918
    B. 1919
    C. 1920
    D. 1921

12. **What was the name of the conference where the Allies planned post-war Europe?**
    A. Paris Peace Conference
    B. Yalta Conference
    C. Potsdam Conference
    D. Tehran Conference

13. **Which city was divided into four occupation zones after World War II?**
    A. Vienna
    B. Paris
    C. Berlin
    D. Warsaw

14. **What was the main purpose of the Lend-Lease Act passed by the United States during World War II?**
    A. To lend money to U.S. allies
    B: To provide military aid to Allied nations
    C. To recruit foreign soldiers for the U.S. Army
    D. To create war bonds

15. **Who was the commander of the Allied forces during the D-Day invasion?**
    A. George S. Patton
    B. Douglas MacArthur
    C. Bernard Montgomery
    D. Dwight D. Eisenhower

Answers Part 2: World Wars

1. C. 1917
2. B. Schlieffen Plan
3. True
4. B. To defend France from Germany
5. A. Battle of Midway
6. B. Erwin Rommel
7. C. 1945
8. B. Operation Dynamo
9. B. Franklin D. Roosevelt
10. A. U-boats
11. B. 1919
12. B. Yalta Conference
13. C. Berlin
14. B. To provide military aid to Allied nations
15. D. Dwight D. Eisenhower

Chapter 18: Science and Technology

Fun Facts About Science and Technology

1. The speed of light is approximately 299,792 kilometres per second (186,282 miles per second), and nothing in the universe can travel faster.
2. The first email was sent by Ray Tomlinson to himself in 1971; he is also credited with using the "@" symbol in email addresses.
3. DNA was first discovered in 1869 by Swiss biologist Friedrich Miescher, but its double-helix structure wasn't identified until 1953 by Watson and Crick.
4. The first programmable computer, called the Zuse Z3, was created in 1941 by Konrad Zuse in Germany.
5. Antibiotics, like penicillin, were discovered accidentally by Alexander Fleming in 1928.
6. The International Space Station (ISS) orbits Earth at a speed of about 28,000 km/h (17,500 mph), completing one orbit every 90 minutes.
7. The human brain generates enough electricity to power a small LED light.
8. The first smartphone, called the IBM Simon, was introduced in 1994, featuring a touchscreen and basic apps.
9. A teaspoon of honey represents the life's work of 12 bees.
10. The internet as we know it started as ARPANET in 1969, a U.S. government project to connect researchers.

Trivia Quiz Part 1: Science and Technology

1. **What is the smallest particle of an element?**
    A. Molecule
    B. Atom
    C. Proton
    D. Electron
2. **Who developed the theory of relativity?**
    A. Isaac Newton
    B. Albert Einstein
    C. Nikola Tesla
    D. Stephen Hawking
3. **True or False: The first artificial satellite in space was launched by the United States.**
4. **What is the name of the process by which plants make their food?**
    A. Respiration
    B. Photosynthesis
    C. Fermentation
    D. Evaporation
5. **What year was the first manned moon landing?**
    A. 1967
    B. 1968
    C. 1969
    D. 1970
6. **What does DNA stand for?**
    A. Deoxyribonucleic Acid
    B. Dynamic Neutron Array
    C. Double Nucleic Acid
    D. Digital Neural Algorithm

7. **What is the unit of electrical resistance?**
   A. Watt
   B. Ampere
   C. Ohm
   D. Volt
8. **Who is known as the father of modern computers?**
   A. Alan Turing
   B. Charles Babbage
   C. John von Neumann
   D. Steve Jobs
9. **What is the primary gas in Earth's atmosphere?**
   A. Oxygen
   B. Carbon Dioxide
   C. Nitrogen
   D. Hydrogen
10. **Which planet is the hottest in the solar system?**
    A. Mercury
    B. Venus
    C. Mars
    D. Jupiter
11. **What is the term for the point in a black hole where gravity is so strong that nothing can escape?**
    A. Singularity
    B. Event Horizon
    C. Gravitational Pull
    D. Schwarzschild Radius

12. **Who invented the telephone?**
    A. Thomas Edison
    B. Alexander Graham Bell
    C. Nikola Tesla
    D. Guglielmo Marconi
13. **What does "AI" stand for in technology?**
    A. Automatic Integration
    B. Artificial Intelligence
    C. Advanced Interface
    D. Algorithmic Insight
14. **What is the main ingredient in traditional glass?**
    A. Sand
    B. Limestone
    C. Clay
    D. Quartz
15. **What is the most abundant element in the universe?**
    A. Oxygen
    B. Hydrogen
    C. Helium
    D. Carbon

Answers Part 1: Science and Technology

1. B. Atom
2. B. Albert Einstein
3. False (It was the Soviet Union with Sputnik 1 in 1957.)
4. B. Photosynthesis
5. C. 1969
6. A. Deoxyribonucleic Acid
7. C. Ohm
8. B. Charles Babbage
9. C. Nitrogen (78% of Earth's atmosphere)
10. B. Venus
11. A. Singularity
12. B. Alexander Graham Bell
13. B. Artificial Intelligence
14. A. Sand
15. B. Hydrogen

Chapter 19: Totally Random Fun Facts

Totally Random and Fascinating Facts

1. Bananas are berries, but strawberries are not.
2. The dot over the lowercase letters "i" and "j" is called a tittle.
3. The shortest war in history was between Britain and Zanzibar in 1896, lasting only 38 minutes.
4. There are more fake flamingos in the world than real ones.
5. Wombat poop is cube-shaped to prevent it from rolling away and to mark their territory.
6. Octopuses have three hearts: two pump blood to the gills, and one pumps it to the rest of the body.
7. A bolt of lightning is five times hotter than the surface of the Sun.
8. The inventor of the Pringles can, Fred Baur, had his ashes buried in one of his cans.
9. The Guinness World Record for the longest hiccupping spree is 68 years.
10. If you shuffle a deck of cards, it's likely that the resulting order has never existed before in history.

Trivia Quiz Part 1: Totally Random Fun Facts

1. **What colour is a polar bear's skin?**
   A. White
   B. Black
   C. Pink
   D. Gray
2. **What is the only continent without ants?**
   A. Europe
   B. Antarctica
   C. Australia
   D. Asia
3. **True or False: Cows have four stomachs.**
4. **What is the smallest country in the world?**
   A. Monaco
   B. Vatican City
   C. San Marino
   D. Liechtenstein
5. **What is the national animal of Scotland?**
   A. Unicorn
   B. Lion
   C. Stag
   D. Wolf
6. **What is the only mammal capable of true flight?**
   A. Squirrel
   B. Bat
   C. Flying Lemur
   D. Gliding Possum
7. **How many hearts does an earthworm have?**
   A. 2
   B. 3
   C. 5
   D. 7

8. **Which fruit floats because it is 25% air?**
    A. Apple
    B. Orange
    C. Watermelon
    D. Pineapple

9. **What is the official term for a fear of long words?**
    A. Hippopotomonstrosesquipedaliophobia
    B. Glossophobia
    C. Sesquipedalophobia
    D. Lexophobia

10. **How long does it take for light to travel from the Sun to Earth?**
    A. 8 seconds
    B. 8 minutes
    C. 8 hours
    D. 8 days

11. **What animal can sleep for up to three years?**
    A. Snail
    B. Tortoise
    C. Bear
    D. Sloth

12. **What is the only food that never spoils?**
    A. Rice
    B. Honey
    C. Salt
    D. Vinegar

13. **What is the world's largest desert?**
    A. Sahara
    B. Gobi
    C. Antarctic Desert
    D. Arabian Desert

14. **Which planet has the most moons in the solar system?**
    A. Saturn
    B. Jupiter
    C. Uranus
    D. Neptune
15. **What is the fear of spiders called?**
    A. Arachnophobia
    B. Entomophobia
    C. Ophidiophobia
    D. Cynophobia

Answers Part 1: Totally Random Fun Facts

1. **B. Black**
2. **B. Antarctica**
3. **True**
4. **B. Vatican City**
5. **A. Unicorn**
6. **B. Bat**
7. **C. 5**
8. **A. Apple**
9. **A. Hippopotomonstrosesquipedaliophobia**
10. **B. 8 minutes**
11. **A. Snail**
12. **B. Honey**
13. **C. Antarctic Desert**
14. **A. Saturn**
15. **A. Arachnophobia**

More Totally Random and Fascinating Facts

1. Koalas sleep up to 22 hours a day, making them one of the sleepiest animals on Earth.
2. The inventor of the frisbee, Ed Headrick, had his ashes moulded into frisbees after his death.
3. The Eiffel Tower can grow up to 6 inches taller in summer due to the expansion of metal in the heat.
4. A group of crows is called a "murder," while a group of owls is called a "parliament."
5. Humans share about 60% of their DNA with bananas.

6. The longest wedding veil was longer than 63 football fields.
7. The shortest war in history, between Britain and Zanzibar, lasted only 38 minutes in 1896.
8. The world's largest snowflake on record was 15 inches wide and 8 inches thick, falling in Montana in 1887.
9. Sloths can hold their breath longer than dolphins—up to 40 minutes—by slowing their heart rate.
10. The longest hiccupping spree lasted for 68 years, starting in 1922.

Trivia Quiz Part 2: Totally Random Fun Facts

1. What is the most common colour of toilet paper in France?
   A. White
   B. Pink
   C. Blue
   D. Yellow
2. Which animal can survive being frozen solid?
   A. Penguin
   B. Wood Frog
   C. Polar Bear
   D. Arctic Fox
3. True or False: The inventor of the lightbulb was Nikola Tesla.
4. What was the first soft drink in space?
   A. Pepsi
   B. Coca-Cola
   C. Sprite
   D. Fanta
5. What is the only letter not used in any U.S. state name?
   A. Q
   B. X
   C. Z
   D. J
6. What is the longest bone in the human body?
   A. Humerus
   B. Femur
   C. Tibia
   D. Radius

7. **Which country consumes the most chocolate per capita?**
   A. Belgium
   B. United States
   C. Switzerland
   D. Germany
8. **What is the fear of heights called?**
   A. Claustrophobia
   B. Agoraphobia
   C. Acrophobia
   D. Ophidiophobia
9. **What is the world's largest island?**
   A. Greenland
   B. Australia
   C. Madagascar
   D. New Guinea
10. **How many noses does a slug have?**
    A. 1
    B. 2
    C. 3
    D. 4
11. **What was the first toy to be advertised on television?**
    A. Yo-Yo
    B. Barbie
    C. Mr. Potato Head
    D. Slinky
12. **What is the national flower of Japan?**
    A. Cherry Blossom
    B. Lotus
    C. Chrysanthemum
    D. Orchid

13. **Which bird can fly backward?**
    A. Hummingbird
    B. Sparrow
    C. Parrot
    D. Kingfisher
14. **What is the world's smallest country?**
    A. Monaco
    B. Liechtenstein
    C. Vatican City
    D. San Marino
15. **What is the strongest muscle in the human body (by size-to-strength ratio)?**
    A. Gluteus Maximus
    B. Masseter (jaw muscle)
    C. Heart
    D. Biceps

Answers Part 2: Totally Random Fun Facts

1. **B. Pink**
2. **B. Wood Frog**
3. **False (It was Thomas Edison.)**
4. **B. Coca-Cola**
5. **A. Q**
6. **B. Femur**
7. **C. Switzerland**
8. **C. Acrophobia**
9. **A. Greenland**
10. **D. 4**
11. **C. Mr. Potato Head**
12. **A. Cherry Blossom**
13. **A. Hummingbird**
14. **C. Vatican City**
15. **B. Masseter (jaw muscle)**

More Unbelievable and Random Facts

1. The fingerprints of a koala are so indistinguishable from humans that they could taint crime scenes.
2. The inventor of Vaseline, Robert Chesebrough, ate a spoonful of it every day and lived to be 96.
3. There's only one letter that doesn't appear in any U.S. state name: the letter "Q."
4. A crocodile can't stick its tongue out.
5. Earth's ozone layer smells faintly of chlorine, while space is often described as having a scent similar to seared steak.

6. The Guinness World Record for the most spoons balanced on a human body is 85.
7. A shrimp's heart is located in its head.
8. If you drive for one hour at 60 mph, you'll travel exactly one degree of latitude.
9. The longest English word has 189,819 letters— it's the full chemical name for the protein nicknamed "titin."
10. The human stomach gets a new lining every three to four days to prevent it from digesting itself.

Trivia Quiz Part 2: Totally Random Fun Facts

1. **What colour was Coca-Cola originally?**
   A. Clear
   B. Red
   C. Green
   D. Black
2. **How many hearts does an octopus have?**
   A. 1
   B. 2
   C. 3
   D. 4
3. **True or False: Humans share 98% of their DNA with chimpanzees.**
4. **What is the only planet that rotates on its side?**
   A. Neptune
   B. Uranus
   C. Venus
   D. Jupiter

5. **What is the fear of clowns called?**
    A. Coulrophobia
    B. Acrophobia
    C. Arachnophobia
    D. Pedophobia
6. **Which animal has the most teeth?**
    A. Crocodile
    B. Snail
    C. Shark
    D. Dolphin
7. **Which food is considered the most stolen item in the world?**
    A. Chocolate
    B. Cheese
    C. Bread
    D. Coffee
8. **What is the official language of Brazil?**
    A. Spanish
    B. Portuguese
    C. English
    D. French
9. **How many colours are there in a rainbow?**
    A. 5
    B. 6
    C. 7
    D. 8
10. **What is the largest type of big cat?**
    A. Lion
    B. Tiger
    C. Jaguar
    D. Leopard

11. Which U.S. city is nicknamed the "Windy City"?
    A. Chicago
    B. Boston
    C. New York
    D. Los Angeles
12. How many legs does a lobster have?
    A. 6
    B. 8
    C. 10
    D. 12
13. What is the capital of Australia?
    A. Sydney
    B. Melbourne
    C. Brisbane
    D. Canberra
14. Which element has the chemical symbol "K"?
    A. Krypton
    B. Potassium
    C. Calcium
    D. Tungsten
15. What is the name of the biggest ocean on Earth?
    A. Atlantic Ocean
    B. Indian Ocean
    C. Pacific Ocean
    D. Arctic Ocean

Answers Part 2: Totally Random Fun Facts

1. C. Green
2. C. 3
3. True
4. B. Uranus
5. A. Coulrophobia
6. B. Snail (They can have over 20,000 teeth.)
7. B. Cheese
8. B. Portuguese
9. C. 7
10. B. Tiger
11. A. Chicago
12. C. 10
13. D. Canberra
14. B. Potassium
15. C. Pacific Ocean

Chapter 20: Human Body

Fascinating Facts About the Human Body

1. The human body contains around 37.2 trillion cells.
2. Your stomach acid is strong enough to dissolve metal, but your stomach protects itself by regenerating its lining every few days.
3. The human brain generates more electrical impulses in a single day than all the telephones in the world combined.
4. The bones in your body make up about 15% of your total body weight.
5. The strongest muscle in the body, by weight-to-strength ratio, is the masseter (jaw muscle).
6. If uncoiled, the DNA in all your body's cells would stretch to Pluto and back (about 6 billion kilometres).
7. Your heart beats about 100,000 times a day, pumping around 2,000 gallons of blood.
8. Fingernails grow faster on your dominant hand and more rapidly in summer than in winter.
9. Babies are born with about 270 bones, but many fuse as they grow, leaving adults with 206 bones.
10. The human liver is the only organ that can regenerate itself, even if 75% of it is damaged.

Trivia Quiz Part 1: Human Body

1. **How many bones are in an adult human body?**
    A. 205
    B. 206
    C. 207
    D. 208
2. **What is the largest organ in the human body?**
    A. Liver
    B. Skin
    C. Brain
    D. Lungs
3. **True or False: Your hair and nails continue to grow after you die.**
4. **What part of the human body contains the most bones?**
    A. Hands
    B. Feet
    C. Spine
    D. Skull
5. **How much blood does the average adult human body contain?**
    A. 4–5 litres
    B. 5–6 litres
    C. 6–7 litres
    D. 7–8 litres
6. **What is the smallest bone in the human body?**
    A. Stapes
    B. Incus
    C. Malleus
    D. Coccyx

7. **Which is the fastest-growing tissue in the human body?**
   A. Hair
   B. Skin
   C. Bone
   D. Fingernails
8. **How many chambers does the human heart have?**
   A. 2
   B. 3
   C. 4
   D. 5
9. **What is the hardest substance in the human body?**
   A. Bone
   B. Enamel
   C. Cartilage
   D. Dentin
10. **What is the average life span of a red blood cell?**
    A. 30 days
    B. 60 days
    C. 90 days
    D. 120 days
11. **What is the name of the pigment that gives skin and hair its colour?**
    A. Keratin
    B. Haemoglobin
    C. Melanin
    D. Collagen

12. **What is the longest muscle in the human body?**
    A. Gluteus Maximus
    B. Sartorius
    C. Biceps
    D. Hamstrings
13. **What is the primary function of platelets in the blood?**
    A. Carry oxygen
    B. Fight infections
    C. Aid in clotting
    D. Regulate body temperature
14. **Which part of the human body is known as the "voice box"?**
    A. Pharynx
    B. Larynx
    C. Trachea
    D. Oesophagus
15. **How many taste buds does the average human tongue have?**
    A. 5,000
    B. 10,000
    C. 15,000
    D. 20,000

Answers Part 1: Human Body

1. B. 206
2. B. Skin
3. False (The appearance of growth is due to skin shrinking after death.)
4. B. Feet (26 bones in each foot)
5. B. 5–6 litres
6. A. Stapes (in the middle ear)
7. D. Fingernails
8. C. 4
9. B. Enamel
10. D. 120 days
11. C. Melanin
12. B. Sartorius
13. C. Aid in clotting
14. B. Larynx
15. B. 10,000

More Fascinating Facts About the Human Body

1. Your body sheds about 30,000 to 40,000 skin cells every minute, which adds up to roughly 9 pounds of skin cells a year.
2. The human brain is about 60% fat, making it the fattiest organ in the body.
3. Your nose can detect over 1 trillion different scents, far more than previously thought.
4. The average human body contains enough iron to make a 3-inch nail.
5. The small intestine is about 22 feet long, making it the longest part of your digestive system.
6. The human eye can distinguish about 10 million different colours.
7. You blink about 15–20 times per minute, which adds up to over 4 million times a year.
8. Sweat itself is odourless; the smell comes from bacteria breaking down the proteins and fatty acids in your sweat.
9. The human body has over 600 muscles, with the gluteus maximus being the largest and the stapedius (in the ear) being the smallest.
10. Your teeth are the only part of your body that cannot repair themselves because they are not made of living tissue.

Trivia Quiz Part 2: Human Body

1. How much of the human body is made up of water?
   A. 50%
   B. 60%
   C. 70%
   D. 80%
2. Which part of the brain controls balance and coordination?
   A. Cerebrum
   B. Cerebellum
   C. Brainstem
   D. Hypothalamus
3. True or False: The average adult has fewer bones than a baby.
4. Which is the largest artery in the human body?
   A. Pulmonary Artery
   B. Coronary Artery
   C. Carotid Artery
   D. Aorta
5. What part of the body produces insulin?
   A. Liver
   B. Pancreas
   C. Kidneys
   D. Spleen
6. Which sense is the last to go when a person dies?
   A. Sight
   B. Hearing
   C. Smell
   D. Touch

7. **What is the average lifespan of a human hair?**
   A. 1–2 years
   B. 2–4 years
   C. 4–7 years
   D. 7–10 years
8. **What is the main function of white blood cells?**
   A. Carry oxygen
   B. Fight infections
   C. Clot blood
   D. Digest food
9. **What is the strongest bone in the human body?**
   A. Skull
   B. Femur
   C. Spine
   D. Jawbone
10. **What organ is responsible for filtering blood?**
    A. Liver
    B. Kidneys
    C. Heart
    D. Spleen
11. **What is the average length of a human pregnancy?**
    A. 36 weeks
    B. 38 weeks
    C. 40 weeks
    D. 42 weeks
12. **Which part of the ear helps with balance?**
    A. Cochlea
    B. Eardrum
    C. Semicircular Canals
    D. Auditory Nerve

13. **How many pints of blood does the human body have?**
    A. 6–7 pints
    B. 8–10 pints
    C. 10–12 pints
    D. 12–14 pints
14. **What percentage of the human brain is water?**
    A. 50%
    B. 60%
    C. 70%
    D. 80%
15. **Which part of the body has the most sweat glands?**
    A. Hands
    B. Feet
    C. Armpits
    D. Face

Answers Part 2: Human Body

1. B. 60%
2. B. Cerebellum
3. True (Babies are born with around 270 bones, which fuse to 206 in adulthood.)
4. D. Aorta
5. B. Pancreas
6. B. Hearing
7. C. 4–7 years
8. B. Fight infections
9. B. Femur
10. B. Kidneys
11. C. 40 weeks
12. C. Semicircular Canals
13. B. 8–10 pints
14. D. 80%
15. B. Feet

More Intriguing Facts About the Human Body

1. Your tongue is made up of eight muscles and is the only muscle in the body that works without being attached to bones.
2. The average human produces enough saliva in a lifetime to fill two swimming pools.
3. Your body has about 100,000 miles of blood vessels, enough to circle the Earth four times.
4. The human nose can remember 50,000 different scents.

5. Goosebumps are a leftover reflex from our ancestors, used to make body hair stand on end to trap heat or appear larger to predators.
6. Your body replaces about 10 billion cells every day.
7. The liver performs over 500 functions, including detoxifying the blood, producing bile, and storing nutrients.
8. Human hair is virtually indestructible, except when burned; it doesn't dissolve in water or decompose easily.
9. The human eye blinks about 20,000 times a day, keeping it moist and free of debris.
10. Bones are about five times stronger than steel of the same density but are brittle and can break under stress.

Trivia Quiz Part 3: Human Body

1. What is the average temperature of the human body?
   A. 96.8°F (36°C)
   B. 97.8°F (36.5°C)
   C. 98.6°F (37°C)
   D. 99.6°F (37.5°C)
2. How many taste buds does the average human tongue have?
   A. 3,000
   B. 5,000
   C. 7,000
   D. 10,000
3. True or False: Your bones are hollow.

4. **What is the largest cell in the human body?**
    A. Brain cell
    B. Egg cell
    C. Liver cell
    D. Muscle cell
5. **What organ has the ability to regenerate itself?**
    A. Lungs
    B. Liver
    C. Heart
    D. Pancreas
6. **Which part of the body has the thinnest skin?**
    A. Eyelids
    B. Lips
    C. Elbows
    D. Wrists
7. **How many bones are in the human hand, including the wrist?**
    A. 24
    B. 27
    C. 29
    D. 32
8. **What percentage of the body's oxygen is used by the brain?**
    A. 10%
    B. 20%
    C. 30%
    D. 40%
9. **What is the main function of the cerebrum in the brain?**
    A. Balance and coordination
    B. Breathing and heart rate

C. Memory and reasoning

D. Hormonal regulation

10. **How many layers of skin does the human body have?**
    A. 2
    B. 3
    C. 4
    D. 5

11. **How many litres of air do humans breathe in a day on average?**
    A. 5,000 litres
    B. 10,000 litres
    C. 15,000 litres
    D. 20,000 litres

12. **Which part of the body produces melatonin?**
    A. Liver
    B. Pineal gland
    C. Thyroid gland
    D. Hypothalamus

13. **What is the heaviest internal organ in the body?**
    A. Brain
    B. Liver
    C. Heart
    D. Lungs

14. **Which part of the eye is responsible for controlling the amount of light that enters?**
    A. Cornea
    B. Retina
    C. Lens
    D. Iris

15. **How many litres of blood does the heart pump every day?**
    A. 2,000 litres
    B. 4,000 litres
    C. 6,000 litres
    D. 8,000 litres

Answers Part 3: Human Body

1. C. 98.6°F (37°C)
2. D. 10,000
3. False (Bones are solid but contain marrow inside.)
4. B. Egg cell
5. B. Liver
6. A. Eyelids
7. B. 27
8. B. 20%
9. C. Memory and reasoning
10. B. 3 (epidermis, dermis, and hypodermis)
11. D. 20,000 litres
12. B. Pineal gland
13. B. Liver (weighing about 3 pounds)
14. D. Iris
15. A. 2,000 litres

Chapter 21: Geography

Fascinating Facts About Geography

1. Mount Everest, the tallest mountain above sea level, is 8,848.86 meters (29,031.7 feet) high, but Mauna Kea in Hawaii is taller if measured from its base underwater.
2. Russia is the largest country in the world, covering over 17 million square kilometres, while Vatican City is the smallest, at just 0.49 square kilometres.
3. The Amazon Rainforest produces 20% of the world's oxygen and spans nine countries in South America.
4. Canada has more lakes than the rest of the world combined.
5. The Dead Sea is the lowest point on Earth, lying about 430 meters (1,412 feet) below sea level.
6. Antarctica is the driest, coldest, and windiest continent, with areas that haven't seen rain in millions of years.
7. Africa is the only continent that stretches across all four hemispheres—northern, southern, eastern, and western.
8. The Nile River in Africa is the longest river in the world, measuring about 6,650 kilometres (4,130 miles).
9. Iceland is the only country in the world without mosquitoes.
10. Australia is home to the Great Barrier Reef, the largest coral reef system on the planet, stretching over 2,300 kilometres (1,429 miles).

Trivia Quiz Part 1: Geography

1. **What is the largest desert in the world?**
   A. Sahara
   B. Gobi
   C. Antarctic Desert
   D. Arabian Desert
2. **What is the capital of Canada?**
   A. Toronto
   B. Ottawa
   C. Vancouver
   D. Montreal
3. **True or False: The Amazon River is the longest river in the world.**
4. **What is the smallest country in the world?**
   A. Monaco
   B. Vatican City
   C. San Marino
   D. Liechtenstein
5. **What is the highest waterfall in the world?**
   A. Victoria Falls
   B. Angel Falls
   C. Niagara Falls
   D. Iguazu Falls
6. **Which country has the most time zones?**
   A. Russia
   B. United States
   C. France
   D. Canada
7. **Which continent has the most countries?**
   A. Asia
   B. Africa
   C. Europe
   D. South America

8. **What is the longest mountain range in the world?**
   A. Andes
   B. Rockies
   C. Himalayas
   D. Alps
9. **What is the deepest ocean in the world?**
   A. Atlantic Ocean
   B. Indian Ocean
   C. Arctic Ocean
   D. Pacific Ocean
10. **What country is known as the "Land of the Rising Sun"?**
    A. China
    B. Japan
    C. Thailand
    D. South Korea
11. **What is the most populous city in the world?**
    A. Tokyo
    B. Shanghai
    C. Delhi
    D. New York
12. **What is the largest island in the world?**
    A. Australia
    B. Greenland
    C. Madagascar
    D. Borneo
13. **What country has the most volcanoes?**
    A. Indonesia
    B. Japan
    C. United States
    D. Philippines

14. **What is the largest freshwater lake by volume?**
    A. Lake Victoria
    B. Lake Superior
    C. Lake Baikal
    D. Lake Tanganyika
15. **Which river flows through Paris?**
    A. Rhine
    B. Seine
    C. Thames
    D. Loire

Answers Part 1: Geography

1. **C. Antarctic Desert**
2. **B. Ottawa**
3. **False** (The Nile is the longest.)
4. **B. Vatican City**
5. **B. Angel Falls**
6. **C. France** (12 time zones due to overseas territories)
7. **B. Africa** (54 countries)
8. **A. Andes**
9. **D. Pacific Ocean**
10. **B. Japan**
11. **A. Tokyo**
12. **B. Greenland**
13. **A. Indonesia**
14. **C. Lake Baikal**
15. **B. Seine**

Even More Fascinating Facts About Geography

1. Mount Everest grows about 4 millimetres each year due to tectonic activity.
2. Lake Baikal in Russia is the deepest and oldest freshwater lake in the world, estimated to be 25 million years old.
3. China shares borders with 14 countries, the most of any nation.
4. The Great Wall of China is not a single wall but a series of walls and fortifications stretching over 13,000 miles.

5. Africa is home to the world's largest desert (Sahara), the longest river (Nile), and the largest waterfall by width (Victoria Falls).
6. The Mariana Trench in the Pacific Ocean is the deepest point on Earth, plunging about 36,000 feet (10,973 meters).
7. Alaska is the westernmost, easternmost, and northernmost state in the U.S. because its Aleutian Islands cross the 180th meridian.
8. Greenland is an autonomous territory of Denmark, not an independent country.
9. Bhutan measures its success in "Gross National Happiness" instead of GDP.
10. The Sahara Desert, the hottest in the world, was a lush, green region with rivers and lakes about 10,000 years ago.

Trivia Quiz Part 2: Geography

1. **What is the largest country in Africa by land area?**
    A. Algeria
    B. Sudan
    C. Democratic Republic of Congo
    D. Libya
2. **What is the capital city of Australia?**
    A. Sydney
    B. Melbourne
    C. Canberra
    D. Brisbane

3. True or False: Europe is the smallest
   continent by land area.
4. Which mountain is known as the "Savage
   Mountain"?
   A. K2
   B. Kilimanjaro
   C. Denali
   D. Annapurna
5. What is the official language of Brazil?
   A. Spanish
   B. English
   C. Portuguese
   D. French
6. What is the smallest ocean in the world?
   A. Indian Ocean
   B. Arctic Ocean
   C. Atlantic Ocean
   D. Southern Ocean
7. Which country is nicknamed the "Emerald
   Isle"?
   A. Iceland
   B. Ireland
   C. Scotland
   D. Wales
8. Which U.S. state is the only one to have a one-
   syllable name?
   A. Maine
   B. Texas
   C. Utah
   D. Ohio

9. **What is the only country that spans two continents?**
   A. Russia
   B. Turkey
   C. Egypt
   D. Kazakhstan

10. **Which river is considered the shortest in the world?**
   A. Roe River
   B. Thames River
   C. Laxford River
   D. Jordan River

11. **What country is home to the Atacama Desert, the driest desert in the world?**
   A. Peru
   B. Chile
   C. Bolivia
   D. Argentina

12. **What European country is known for having more than 400 islands?**
   A. Norway
   B. Sweden
   C. Denmark
   D. Finland

13. **Which African lake is the largest by surface area?**
   A. Lake Malawi
   B. Lake Victoria
   C. Lake Tanganyika
   D. Lake Chad

14. **What is the tallest volcano on Earth?**
    A. Mount Etna
    B. Mount Kilimanjaro
    C. Mauna Kea
    D. Mount Vesuvius
15. **What country is known as the "Land of a Thousand Lakes"?**
    A. Norway
    B. Canada
    C. Finland
    D. Sweden

Answers Part 2: Geography

1. A. Algeria
2. C. Canberra
3. False (Australia is the smallest continent.)
4. A. K2
5. C. Portuguese
6. B. Arctic Ocean
7. B. Ireland
8. A. Maine
9. B. Turkey
10. A. Roe River (61 meters/200 feet long)
11. B. Chile
12. C. Denmark
13. B. Lake Victoria
14. C. Mauna Kea (when measured from its base underwater)
15. C. Finland

Chapter 22: Natural Wonders

Fascinating Facts About Natural Wonders

1. The Grand Canyon in the United States is over 277 miles long, up to 18 miles wide, and a mile deep, with rock layers that are billions of years old.
2. Mount Everest, the highest point on Earth above sea level, rises by about 4 millimetres each year due to tectonic activity.
3. The Amazon Rainforest produces 20% of the world's oxygen and is home to over 10% of all known species on Earth.
4. Victoria Falls, located on the border of Zambia and Zimbabwe, is known locally as "The Smoke That Thunders."
5. The Great Barrier Reef in Australia is the largest coral reef system in the world, stretching over 2,300 kilometres (1,429 miles).
6. The Dead Sea, the lowest point on Earth, has such high salinity that people naturally float on its surface.
7. Yellowstone National Park, located in the U.S., sits atop a super volcano capable of producing eruptions thousands of times more powerful than Mount St. Helens.
8. Uluru (Ayers Rock) in Australia is a massive sandstone monolith that changes colour depending on the time of day and weather conditions.
9. The Aurora Borealis (Northern Lights) is caused by charged particles from the Sun colliding with Earth's atmosphere.

10. The Salar de Uyuni in Bolivia is the world's largest salt flat and reflects the sky like a giant mirror when covered with water.

Trivia Quiz Part 1: Natural Wonders

1. **What is the tallest waterfall in the world?**
   A. Niagara Falls
   B. Angel Falls
   C. Victoria Falls
   D. Iguazu Falls
2. **Which mountain is the tallest in the world above sea level?**
   A. Mount Everest
   B. K2
   C. Mount Kilimanjaro
   D. Denali
3. **True or False: The Great Barrier Reef is visible from space.**
4. **What is the largest rainforest in the world?**
   A. Congo Rainforest
   B. Amazon Rainforest
   C. Daintree Rainforest
   D. Sundarbans
5. **What natural phenomenon is caused by the interaction of solar wind with Earth's magnetic field?**
   A. Tsunamis
   B. Earthquakes
   C. Aurora Borealis
   D. Hurricanes

6. **Which desert is the hottest in the world?**
   A. Gobi Desert
   B. Sahara Desert
   C. Mojave Desert
   D. Kalahari Desert
7. **Where is the world's largest cave located?**
   A. Vietnam
   B. Brazil
   C. China
   D. Australia
8. **Which natural wonder is also known as "The Door to Hell"?**
   A. Mount Etna
   B. Darvaza Gas Crater
   C. Yellowstone Caldera
   D. Mount Vesuvius
9. **What is the largest glacier in the world?**
   A. Lambert Glacier
   B. Perito Moreno Glacier
   C. Vatnajökull Glacier
   D. Fox Glacier
10. **Which lake is the deepest in the world?**
    A. Lake Superior
    B. Lake Victoria
    C. Lake Baikal
    D. Lake Tanganyika
11. **What is the name of the rock formation in Arizona that creates a "wave" pattern?**
    A. Monument Valley
    B. The Wave
    C. Horseshoe Bend
    D. Antelope Canyon

12. Which continent is home to the tallest free-standing mountain in the world?
    A. Asia
    B. Africa
    C. South America
    D. North America
13. What is the largest coral reef system in the world?
    A. Great Barrier Reef
    B. Belize Barrier Reef
    C. New Caledonian Barrier Reef
    D. Red Sea Coral Reef
14. Which country is home to the Marble Caves, known for their vibrant colours?
    A. Peru
    B. Chile
    C. Argentina
    D. Bolivia
15. What is the name of the natural wonder in Iceland known for erupting hot water and steam?
    A. Geysir
    B. Strokkur
    C. Thingvellir
    D. Gullfoss

Answers Part 1: Natural Wonders

1. B. Angel Falls
2. A. Mount Everest
3. True
4. B. Amazon Rainforest
5. C. Aurora Borealis
6. B. Sahara Desert
7. A. Vietnam (Hang Sơn Đoòng)
8. B. Darvaza Gas Crater
9. A. Lambert Glacier
10. C. Lake Baikal
11. B. The Wave
12. B. Africa (Mount Kilimanjaro)
13. A. Great Barrier Reef
14. B. Chile
15. A. Geysir

Even More Fascinating Facts About Natural Wonders

1. The Amazon River discharges approximately 209,000 cubic meters of water per second into the Atlantic Ocean, making it the river with the greatest flow rate in the world.
2. The Dead Sea is nearly 10 times saltier than the ocean, making it inhospitable to most life forms but ideal for floating effortlessly.
3. The Great Blue Hole in Belize is a giant marine sinkhole, about 318 meters (1,043 feet) across and 124 meters (407 feet) deep.

4. The Marble Caves in Patagonia, Chile, were formed over 6,000 years ago by waves eroding the calcium carbonate into stunning blue and white swirls.
5. The Atacama Desert in Chile is the driest place on Earth, with some areas that haven't seen rain in recorded history.
6. The Northern Lights (Aurora Borealis) have a southern counterpart called the Aurora Australis, visible from Antarctica, Australia, and southern South America.
7. Mount Roraima, located in Venezuela, Brazil, and Guyana, is a tabletop mountain that inspired the setting for Arthur Conan Doyle's novel *The Lost World*.
8. The Cliffs of Moher in Ireland rise 214 meters (702 feet) above the Atlantic Ocean and attract over a million visitors annually.
9. Iguazu Falls, located on the border between Brazil and Argentina, consists of 275 waterfalls, making it one of the largest waterfall systems in the world.
10. The Giant's Causeway in Northern Ireland is made up of about 40,000 interlocking basalt columns formed by volcanic activity millions of years ago.

Trivia Quiz Part 2: Natural Wonders

1. **What is the name of the world's largest salt flat?**
   A. Bonneville Salt Flats
   B. Salar de Uyuni
   C. Etosha Pan
   D. Danakil Depression
2. **Which country is home to Mount Fitz Roy, also known as Cerro Chaltén?**
   A. Argentina
   B. Peru
   C. Chile
   D. Bolivia
3. **True or False: The Dead Sea is shrinking due to reduced water inflow and high evaporation rates.**
4. **What is the name of the world's largest active volcano?**
   A. Mount St. Helens
   B. Kilauea
   C. Mauna Loa
   D. Mount Etna
5. **Which natural wonder in New Zealand is known for its colourful geothermal pools?**
   A. Milford Sound
   B. Wai-O-Tapu Thermal Wonderland
   C. Franz Josef Glacier
   D. Tongariro National Park

6. **Which river forms the border between Zambia and Zimbabwe?**
   A. Congo River
   B. Nile River
   C. Zambezi River
   D. Limpopo River

7. **What natural phenomenon causes geysers to erupt?**
   A. Earthquakes
   B. Volcanic activity
   C. Heat from magma
   D. Water pressure underground

8. **What is the largest canyon in the world by volume?**
   A. Grand Canyon
   B. Copper Canyon
   C. Yarlung Tsangpo Grand Canyon
   D. Fish River Canyon

9. **What is the name of the underwater waterfall located near Mauritius?**
   A. Challenger Deep
   B. Oceanic Trench
   C. Submarine Cataract
   D. Underwater Waterfall Illusion

10. **What is the largest waterfall by water flow in the world?**
    A. Angel Falls
    B. Victoria Falls
    C. Boyoma Falls
    D. Niagara Falls

11. **What mountain range is home to the Matterhorn?**
    A. Andes
    B. Rockies
    C. Alps
    D. Himalayas
12. **What is the name of the largest hot desert in the world?**
    A. Gobi Desert
    B. Mojave Desert
    C. Kalahari Desert
    D. Sahara Desert
13. **What country is home to the Plitvice Lakes National Park, known for its cascading lakes and waterfalls?**
    A. Slovenia
    B. Croatia
    C. Bosnia
    D. Montenegro
14. **What is the name of the towering rock spires in Utah's Bryce Canyon National Park?**
    A. Hoodoos
    B. Pinnacles
    C. Spires
    D. Columns
15. **Which natural wonder in Africa is known for its pink-hued flamingo populations?**
    A. Lake Victoria
    B. Lake Nakuru
    C. Lake Malawi
    D. Lake Tanganyika

Answers Part 2: Natural Wonders

1. B. Salar de Uyuni
2. A. Argentina
3. True
4. C. Mauna Loa
5. B. Wai-O-Tapu Thermal Wonderland
6. C. Zambezi River
7. D. Water pressure underground
8. C. Yarlung Tsangpo Grand Canyon
9. D. Underwater Waterfall Illusion
10. C. Boyoma Falls
11. C. Alps
12. D. Sahara Desert
13. B. Croatia
14. A. Hoodoos
15. B. Lake Nakuru

Chapter 23: Religions

Fascinating Facts About Religions

1. Hinduism is the oldest known organised religion, dating back over 4,000 years.
2. Christianity is the largest religion in the world, with over 2.3 billion followers.
3. Islam is the fastest-growing religion in the world and has over 1.9 billion adherents.
4. The Dalai Lama is considered the spiritual leader of Tibetan Buddhism and is believed to be a reincarnation of previous Dalai Lamas.
5. Judaism, Christianity, and Islam are known as the Abrahamic religions because they trace their origins to the patriarch Abraham.
6. Sikhism, founded in the 15th century in Punjab, India, emphasises equality, service, and devotion to one God.
7. The Bible is the best-selling book of all time, with billions of copies sold.
8. The Quran, the holy book of Islam, is written in classical Arabic and believed by Muslims to be the word of God as revealed to Prophet Muhammad.
9. The lotus flower is a symbol of purity and enlightenment in Buddhism.
10. Confucianism, originating in China, is more of a philosophical and ethical system than a religion, emphasising morality and social harmony.

Trivia Quiz Part 1: Religions

1. **What is the largest religion in the world by number of adherents?**
   A. Islam
   B. Christianity
   C. Hinduism
   D. Buddhism
2. **What is the sacred text of Hinduism?**
   A. Torah
   B. Quran
   C. Vedas
   D. Tripitaka
3. **True or False: Judaism is the oldest monotheistic religion.**
4. **What is the religious symbol associated with Buddhism?**
   A. Crescent Moon
   B. Cross
   C. Lotus Flower
   D. Star of David
5. **Which religion celebrates Diwali, the festival of lights?**
   A. Hinduism
   B. Buddhism
   C. Sikhism
   D. All of the above
6. **What is the place of worship for Muslims called?**
   A. Church
   B. Temple
   C. Synagogue
   D. Mosque

7. **Who is the founder of Buddhism?**
   A. Confucius
   B. Siddhartha Gautama
   C. Guru Nanak
   D. Laozi
8. **Which religion observes Yom Kippur, the Day of Atonement?**
   A. Islam
   B. Christianity
   C. Judaism
   D. Zoroastrianism
9. **What is the sacred river in Hinduism?**
   A. Ganges
   B. Nile
   C. Amazon
   D. Indus
10. **What is the primary holy book of Sikhism?**
    A. Bhagavad Gita
    B. Quran
    C. Guru Granth Sahib
    D. Bible
11. **Which religion is known for its Eightfold Path to enlightenment?**
    A. Christianity
    B. Islam
    C. Hinduism
    D. Buddhism
12. **What is the holiest city in Islam?**
    A. Medina
    B. Mecca
    C. Jerusalem
    D. Cairo

13. **Which religion uses the Torah as its sacred text?**
    A. Judaism
    B. Christianity
    C. Islam
    D. Zoroastrianism
14. **What is the main symbol of Sikhism?**
    A. Om
    B. Khanda
    C. Crescent Moon
    D. Lotus Flower
15. **Who is considered the last prophet in Islam?**
    A. Abraham
    B. Jesus
    C. Muhammad
    D. Moses

Answers Part 1: Religions

1. B. Christianity
2. C. Vedas
3. True
4. C. Lotus Flower
5. D. All of the above
6. D. Mosque
7. B. Siddhartha Gautama
8. C. Judaism
9. A. Ganges
10. C. Guru Granth Sahib
11. D. Buddhism
12. B. Mecca
13. A. Judaism
14. B. Khanda
15. C. Muhammad

Even More Fascinating Facts About Religions

1. The word "Islam" means "submission" in Arabic, reflecting the faith's emphasis on submission to God's will
2. Hinduism is unique in having no single founder, and it encompasses a diverse range of beliefs and practices.
3. The Buddhist Wheel of Dharma has eight spokes, representing the Noble Eightfold Path.
4. Judaism introduced the concept of a weekly day of rest, the Sabbath, which is observed from Friday evening to Saturday evening.

5. Christianity was legalised in the Roman Empire by Emperor Constantine in 313 CE with the Edict of Milan.
6. The Kaaba in Mecca is considered the most sacred site in Islam, and Muslims around the world pray in its direction.
7. Zoroastrianism, one of the world's oldest religions, originated in ancient Persia and influenced later Abrahamic religions.
8. Shinto, the indigenous religion of Japan, revolves around the worship of kami (spirits) in nature and ancestors.
9. Jainism, an ancient Indian religion, emphasises non-violence to all living beings and practices strict vegetarianism.
10. The Sikh turban, or dastar, is worn as a symbol of equality and honour, and cutting hair is discouraged as it is seen as a gift from God.

Trivia Quiz Part 2: Religions

1. **What is the largest branch of Christianity?**
    A. Protestantism
    B. Roman Catholicism
    C. Eastern Orthodoxy
    D. Anglicanism
2. **What is the name of the Islamic month of fasting?**
    A. Shawwal
    B. Rajab
    C. Ramadan
    D. Dhul-Hijjah
3. **True or False: Buddhism is a polytheistic religion.**
4. **What is the holiest site in Judaism?**
    A. Dome of the Rock
    B. Western Wall
    C. Mount Sinai
    D. Masada
5. **Which religion celebrates Vesak, commemorating the birth, enlightenment, and death of its founder?**
    A. Jainism
    B. Buddhism
    C. Sikhism
    D. Shinto
6. **Which sacred text contains the teachings of Confucius?**
    A. Tao Te Ching
    B. The Analects
    C. Tripitaka
    D. Rigveda

7. **What is the name of the Hindu festival of colours?**
   A. Diwali
   B. Navratri
   C. Holi
   D. Pongal

8. **Who is the main god in Zoroastrianism?**
   A. Zeus
   B. Ahura Mazda
   C. Odin
   D. Brahma

9. **Which religion believes in the Four Noble Truths?**
   A. Hinduism
   B. Jainism
   C. Buddhism
   D. Taoism

10. **What is the primary symbol of Christianity?**
    A. Cross
    B. Star
    C. Crescent Moon
    D. Lotus Flower

11. **Which religion believes in the concept of Yin and Yang?**
    A. Shinto
    B. Taoism
    C. Confucianism
    D. Zoroastrianism

12. **What is the central teaching of Jainism?**
    A. Meditation
    B. Non-violence
    C. Enlightenment
    D. Karma

13. **Which country has the largest Muslim population in the world?**
    A. Saudi Arabia
    B. Indonesia
    C. Pakistan
    D. India
14. **What is the sacred text of Sikhism?**
    A. Guru Granth Sahib
    B. Bhagavad Gita
    C. Quran
    D. Bible
15. **What religion has a sacred symbol called the "Om"?**
    A. Buddhism
    B. Hinduism
    C. Sikhism
    D. Taoism

Answers Part 2: Religions

1. B. Roman Catholicism
2. C. Ramadan
3. False (Buddhism is non-theistic.)
4. B. Western Wall
5. B. Buddhism
6. B. The Analects
7. C. Holi
8. B. Ahura Mazda
9. C. Buddhism
10. A. Cross
11. B. Taoism
12. B. Non-violence
13. B. Indonesia
14. A. Guru Granth Sahib
15. B. Hinduism

Chapter 24: Mythology

Fascinating Facts About Mythology

1. Greek mythology is one of the most well-known mythologies and features gods like Zeus, Poseidon, and Hades, who ruled the skies, seas, and underworld, respectively.
2. Norse mythology tells of nine realms connected by Yggdrasil, the World Tree, with Asgard as the home of the gods like Odin and Thor.
3. Egyptian mythology includes deities such as Ra, the sun god, and Anubis, the god of mummification, who were central to their beliefs about the afterlife.
4. The ancient Roman gods closely mirrored Greek gods but had different names, such as Jupiter for Zeus and Neptune for Poseidon.
5. In Hindu mythology, Lord Vishnu is believed to have 10 avatars, including Rama and Krishna, who descended to restore cosmic order.
6. Chinese mythology includes the Jade Emperor as the ruler of Heaven and Earth, along with stories of mythical creatures like dragons and phoenixes.
7. The Aztecs worshipped a sun god named Huitzilopochtli, and human sacrifice was a common practice to ensure the sun continued to rise.
8. Japanese mythology features Amaterasu, the sun goddess, and Susanoo, the storm god, who are part of the Shinto pantheon.

9. The Maori of New Zealand believe in gods like Tane Mahuta, the god of forests, and Maui, who is said to have fished up the North Island.
10. The Epic of Gilgamesh from Mesopotamian mythology is one of the oldest written stories in the world, telling the tale of a king seeking immortality.

Trivia Quiz Part 1: Mythology

1. Who is the king of the gods in Greek mythology?
   A. Hades
   B. Zeus
   C. Poseidon
   D. Apollo
2. What is the name of Thor's hammer in Norse mythology?
   A. Gungnir
   B. Mjölnir
   C. Excalibur
   D. Durandal
3. True or False: The Egyptian god Anubis is associated with the sun.
4. Which Roman god is equivalent to the Greek god Hermes?
   A. Apollo
   B. Mercury
   C. Mars
   D. Vulcan

5. **What is the name of the river that separates the living from the dead in Greek mythology?**
   A. Styx
   B. Lethe
   C. Acheron
   D. Cocytus

6. **Who is the Hindu god of destruction and transformation?**
   A. Vishnu
   B. Shiva
   C. Brahma
   D. Krishna

7. **What creature is part lion, part eagle in mythology?**
   A. Chimera
   B. Griffin
   C. Sphinx
   D. Pegasus

8. **In Japanese mythology, who is the sun goddess?**
   A. Tsukuyomi
   B. Amaterasu
   C. Susanoo
   D. Izanami

9. **What is the name of the serpent in Norse mythology that encircles the world?**
   A. Fenrir
   B. Jörmungandr
   C. Nidhogg
   D. Fafnir

10. What is the name of the first woman in Greek mythology, created by Hephaestus?
    A. Persephone
    B. Pandora
    C. Aphrodite
    D. Hera
11. Which culture believed in a feathered serpent god named Quetzalcoatl?
    A. Inca
    B. Aztec
    C. Mayan
    D. Maori
12. What is the name of the Greek goddess of wisdom?
    A. Athena
    B. Hera
    C. Artemis
    D. Demeter
13. Which Egyptian god has a falcon head and is associated with the sky?
    A. Horus
    B. Ra
    C. Osiris
    D. Set
14. In Norse mythology, who is the trickster god?
    A. Loki
    B. Odin
    C. Thor
    D. Balder

15. **What is the name of the hero in the ancient Mesopotamian epic?**
    A. Gilgamesh
    B. Enkidu
    C. Hammurabi
    D. Sargon

Answers Part 1: Mythology

1. B. Zeus
2. B. Mjölnir
3. False (Anubis is associated with mummification and the afterlife.)
4. B. Mercury
5. A. Styx
6. B. Shiva
7. B. Griffin
8. B. Amaterasu
9. B. Jörmungandr
10. B. Pandora
11. B. Aztec
12. A. Athena
13. A. Horus
14. A. Loki
15. A. Gilgamesh

Even More Fascinating Facts About Mythology

1. The Greek myth of Icarus warns of the dangers of hubris; he flew too close to the sun, melting the wax in his wings, and fell into the sea.
2. Ragnarok in Norse mythology is the prophesied end of the world, a great battle where many gods, including Odin and Thor, will meet their demise.
3. In Egyptian mythology, the goddess Ma'at weighs the hearts of the dead against a feather to determine their fate in the afterlife.

4. The Hindu epic *Mahabharata* is the longest epic poem ever written, containing over 100,000 verses.
5. The Chinese zodiac, used in Chinese mythology, consists of 12 animal signs, including the dragon, which is the only mythical creature.
6. In Celtic mythology, the Morrigan is a goddess associated with war, fate, and death, often appearing as a crow.
7. The Aztec calendar stone, often mistaken for a depiction of their calendar, is actually a representation of their cosmological beliefs.
8. In Japanese folklore, Kitsune (foxes) are magical creatures capable of shapeshifting into humans, often acting as messengers for the gods.
9. The Mayan creation myth, *Popol Vuh*, tells the story of twin heroes who journey to the underworld to defeat the gods of death.
10. In Greek mythology, the Labyrinth was built by Daedalus to imprison the Minotaur, a creature that was half-man and half-bull.

Trivia Quiz Part 2: Mythology

1. Who is the Greek god of the sea?
   A. Zeus
   B. Hades
   C. Poseidon
   D. Apollo
2. What is the Norse realm of the dead, ruled by Hel, called?
   A. Valhalla
   B. Helheim
   C. Jotunheim
   D. Alfheim
3. True or False: The Egyptian god Osiris is the god of the underworld.
4. Which creature in Greek mythology has snakes for hair and turns people to stone?
   A. Sphinx
   B. Medusa
   C. Hydra
   D. Chimera
5. What is the Hindu festival that celebrates the victory of good over evil, light over darkness?
   A. Holi
   B. Diwali
   C. Navratri
   D. Pongal
6. Which Roman god is the equivalent of the Greek god Ares?
   A. Apollo
   B. Mars
   C. Mercury
   D. Pluto

7. **What is the name of the Japanese sun goddess who hid in a cave, plunging the world into darkness?**
   A. Amaterasu
   B. Tsukuyomi
   C. Susanoo
   D. Izanagi

8. **What is the name of the serpent slain by Thor during Ragnarok?**
   A. Fenrir
   B. Nidhogg
   C. Jörmungandr
   D. Fafnir

9. **Who is the Celtic god of the sea and healing?**
   A. Lugh
   B. Dagda
   C. Manannán mac Lir
   D. Cernunnos

10. **What is the name of the hero who sailed on the Argo to retrieve the Golden Fleece?**
    A. Hercules
    B. Perseus
    C. Jason
    D. Theseus

11. **Which creature is said to guard the gates of the underworld in Greek mythology?**
    A. Cerberus
    B. Charon
    C. Hydra
    D. Pegasus

12. In Norse mythology, what is the name of the hall where warriors slain in battle are taken?
    A. Vanaheim
    B. Valhalla
    C. Helheim
    D. Midgard
13. Which Aztec god was known as the god of rain and agriculture?
    A. Quetzalcoatl
    B. Huitzilopochtli
    C. Tezcatlipoca
    D. Tlaloc
14. What is the name of the Greek goddess of the harvest?
    A. Hera
    B. Athena
    C. Demeter
    D. Artemis
15. In Chinese mythology, what creature is believed to bring luck and prosperity?
    A. Dragon
    B. Phoenix
    C. Unicorn
    D. Tiger

Answers Part 2: Mythology

1. C. Poseidon
2. B. Helheim
3. True
4. B. Medusa
5. B. Diwali
6. B. Mars
7. A. Amaterasu
8. C. Jörmungandr
9. C. Manannán mac Lir
10. C. Jason
11. A. Cerberus
12. B. Valhalla
13. D. Tlaloc
14. C. Demeter
15. A. Dragon